Other
Worlds

Other Worlds

Society Seen Through Soap Opera

DOROTHY ANGER

broadview press

©1999 Dorothy Anger

Canadian Cataloguing in Publication Data

Anger, Dorothy C. (Dorothy Catherine), 1954–   .
  Other worlds : society seen through soap opera

ISBN 1-55111-103-9
1. Soap operas — Social aspects — United States. 2. Soap operas — Social aspects — Great Britain. I. Title.

PN1992.8.S4A533 1998   791.45'6   C98-932270-X

Broadview Press Ltd., is an independent, international publishing house, incorporated in 1985.

North America:
P.O. Box 1243, Peterborough, Ontario, Canada K9J 7H5
3576 California Road, Orchard Park, NY 14127
TEL: (705) 743-8990; FAX: (705) 743-8353;
E-MAIL: 75322.44@compuserve.com

United Kingdom:
Turpin Distribution Services Ltd.,
Blackhorse Rd., Letchworth, Hertfordshire SG6 1HN
TEL: (1462) 672555; FAX (1462) 480947; E-MAIL: turpin@rsc.org

Australia:
St. Clair Press, P.O. Box 287, Rozelle, NSW 2039
TEL: (02) 818-1942; FAX: (02) 418-1923

www.broadviewpress.com

Broadview Press gratefully acknowledges the financial support of the Book Publishing Industry Development Program, Ministry of Canadian Heritage, Government of Canada.

.

Composition by George Kirkpatrick.

PRINTED

To my parents, George and Ruby Anger

Contents

Preface

We do not live in this world alone, but in a thousand other worlds. The events of our lives represent only the surface, and in our minds and feelings we live in many other worlds.

ORIGINAL OPENING WORDS OF ANOTHER WORLD

There was a book a few years ago ... which purported to trace all the influences that had led me into writing [Coronation Street]. It took five of them to do it, and it took one of me to write it, and this one couldn't understand what they were going on about....I've read criticism of Coronation Street that has sent me running to the dictionary, and still been none the wiser. People have tried to turn it into something more important than what it is. It's entertainment....They run the risk of spoiling it. Some of the questions you've asked me, I wonder if you'd ask a conjurer how his illusions work!

TONY WARREN, CREATOR OF CORONATION STREET,
IN AN INTERVIEW WITH THE AUTHOR

Acknowledgements

MANY people have helped me with this project from its inception as a radio documentary to a university course and now a book. *Ideas*, the national CBC Radio documentary programme, provided the opportunity and means for me to research soaps on both sides of the Atlantic. Special thanks to executive-producer Bernie Lucht and St. John's producer Maureen Anonsen. Many soap actors, producers, technicians, publicists, and magazine editors in New York and throughout England went out of their way to help me, and for this I thank them all.

Don LePan, publisher of Broadview Press, suggested I write a book on this topic. I thank him for this and for the unfailing support he and co-publisher Michael Harrison have given me. The production and editorial assistance of Barbara Conolly, Betsy Struthers, and Terry Teskey has been invaluable. They cheerfully kept the project on track despite some considerable logistical nightmares.

I thank Dr. Priscilla Renouf, former head of the Anthropology Department at Memorial University, and Department Secretary Marilyn Marshall for encouraging me to develop the material into a popular culture course and ensuring that I did it. Faculty and staff of the Anthropology and Sociology Departments and the School of Continuing Education have given every assistance and support to me.

Friends and mentors George and Alice Park and Chris Brookes read early drafts of the manuscript, and their comments were of great help in clarifying and improving it. Other friends contributed to the book and my life, among them Geralyn Lynch, the O'Brien family, Gary Wilton, Judy Dwyer, Vince Walsh, Marilyn Snow, and Michael Finlay. Thank you.

I am truly gratified for the constant support I receive from my parents, sister Onalee Ogglesby, brother Allan Anger, and their families.

Cedric and Jamie were my four-footed advisors during most of this writing. When they passed away, Elsie and Jack took on the job. They have been assisted by Doug, Spam, and Sid.

Thanks to all who gave me their thoughts on the business of story-telling. Without those insights, I would not have learned about the world of soaps. However, responsibility for errors and inaccuracies is solely mine.

"Bingo and *Another World*" is reprinted courtesy of the estate of Rex Hemeon. Drumhead Music, 1979.

Notes to the Text

Direct quotations in the text when not referenced to a printed source or interview are from personal comments made to the author in conversation with various anonymous sources.

The roles of actors and the positions of writers, producers, and other personnel were accurate at time of interviews.

The Soaps

American:

ABC

All My Children AMC
General Hospital GH
One Life to Live OLTL
Port Charles

CBS

As the World Turns ATWT (Procter & Gamble)
The Bold and the Beautiful B&B (Columbia Tri-Star/Bell-Phillip Productions)
Guiding Light GL (Procter & Gamble)
The Young and the Restless Y&R (Columbia Tri-Star, Bell-Phillip Productions)

NBC

Another World AW (Procter & Gamble)
Days of Our Lives DOOL (Corday Productions)
Sunset Beach (Aaron Spelling Productions)

Magazines

Soap Opera Digest SOD
Soap Opera Weekly SOW

British:

Brookside (Channel 4)
Coronation Street CS (Granada Television)
EastEnders EE (BBC)
Emmerdale (Yorkshire Television)

One
Introduction: The History of the Soaps

WHEN I was young, I wanted to spend my precious after-school hours hanging out on street corners. My girlfriends disappointed me bitterly; they raced home from school to watch *The Edge of Night*. I thought watching soaps was a foolish waste of time.

My time was to come; I became hooked on soaps slowly. In 1978, newly minted anthropology B.A. in hand, I took a position working with a First Nations council in northern British Columbia. I learned my first fieldwork lesson when I realized I hadn't a hope of taking part in conversations if I didn't know *Another World*'s Bay City, for the people I was interviewing interspersed talk about *AW*'s characters with comments on events in their own town. I was welcome in their homes when "the story" was on if I wanted to watch, but not if I wanted to interview them. I forgot Bay City when I left that community, but met with it again the following year when I worked in a small town in Newfoundland. The stories were equally important there. *AW* and *General Hospital* were the soaps of choice in the house where I boarded. This time when I finished my work and left the community, I didn't leave Bay City or Port Charles behind. I could no longer justify watching the stories as a demand of fieldwork; now, transparently, I just wanted to know what was happening. I'd taken the bait and was hooked.

My admission that I watched soaps was received incredulously by friends. But some of those friends had more knowledge of soaps than a true non-viewer could plausibly possess. That inconsistency, and the fans who in conversation came out of the closet, drew my interest, drew me to what I think of as the underworld of soap watching: the role of soaps in facilitating conversation between strangers and in shaping conversation between friends. I can attest to its power in my own life: in the course of my research on soaps I learned that my own sister had long been a follower of *GH*. Thereafter we kept phone companies and ourselves happy discussing long-distance what was happening and might happen in Port Charles and environs.

Via my "research," I now know the denizens of five American soaps plus the British serial *Coronation Street*, and soap opera magazines familiarize me with American soaps I don't watch. Sometimes they bore me, annoy me, insult my intelligence, but still I watch: to see what happens next, even to see just how outrageous a story will get.

There is no one particular literary, sociological, or industry perspective shaping this examination of soap operas. (Many excellent books do adopt such perspectives, and this one can point interested readers in their direction.) I am instead eclectic in my approach, borrowing what seems insightful here and there and leaving the reader to decide what is of most use to him or her. I do have one fixed "point of reference," if it can be called that: I write from an *engaged* perspective. I enjoy the soaps.

I define soaps as programmes:

    a)   consisting of multiple storylines which continue from episode to episode,

    b)   for which an eventual end is neither foreseen nor written toward,

    c)   which air more than once weekly, and

    d)   which derive their story content primarily from emotion and affairs of the heart.[1]

Taken together, these four elements distinguish soaps from such North American "prime-time serials" as *Dallas, Melrose Place, Party of Five, ER, NYPD Blues, North of 60, Traders*, and so on. Beginning with *Hill Street Blues* in the 1980s, such prime-time episodic series adopted the trend of continuing plotlines from episode to episode without immediate resolution and maintaining a relatively stable ensemble cast. The writers of these shows learned what soaps writers have long known—audiences do not necessarily want quick, tidy resolutions and like to be hooked on "what happens next."

In the following chapters, I look at the history and development of soap operas, often using either American or British serials to illustrate their salient aspects. I compare British and American techniques of production, especially in their concern for and understanding of "realism." The vision of society presented, intentionally and unintentionally, by American and British serials is analyzed in terms of national ethos and understanding of physical and social "place." The viewer, of course, is included in these discussions either implicitly or explicitly, and a later chapter is devoted entirely to the relationship between these fictional worlds and their real-life audiences.

My intent in these pages is to introduce readers to the study of soaps as cultural products and processes by comparing US daytime drama and British continuing serials (the labels preferred by the respective industries). I have been told that comparing the two is like comparing chalk and cheese. Granted, they are greatly dissimilar in many respects; but in their formal elements—their longevity, unending nature, and basis in daily and family life—as well as in their popularity they do bear comparison. My circumstances of work and soap watching have caused me to think about how soaps are made, how what they say reflects the society in which they are made, and how they are received and used by viewers.

★   ★   ★

Soap operas, or continuing serials, have been part of television since its inception in the US and soon thereafter in the UK. Before the advent of television, soaps existed on radio. Further back, in the seventeenth and eighteenth centuries, works of literature were published in instalments—that is, in serial form—making them less expensive to print and so affordable to more buyers. In the nineteenth century serial publication of new novels became popular in Britain with the appearance of Charles Dickens's *Pickwick Papers* (1836) and in France with Eugène Sue's *Les mystères de Paris* (1842). Authors such as Trollope, Hardy, Dumas, and Zola followed suit with serialization in magazines and newspapers (Hagedorn 1995: 29-31). The practice of serialization has, in short, a long and honourable pedigree.

Serials appeal to us because we like storytelling, and we want to know what happens next. Novels, movies, and television series end. For all of us who have ever walked out of a movie theatre or put down a novel and said, "I wonder what happens now?," continuing serials are the answer to our desire to know more.

In American and British soaps an end is not written towards, although low audience ratings may result in cancellation and hence the need to impose some sort of closure. Still, when cancellation occurs, the loose ends of all the stories are not, indeed normally could not, be tied up.[2] It is the never-ending nature of soap opera that is its dominant defining characteristic. This is a part of what Robert Allan defines as "open" serials in contrast to "closed" serials, in which closure will eventually occur (1995: 18-24). In the *telenovelas* of Latin America and *teleromans* of Quebec, an end is planned, even if it is years and hundreds of episodes in the future. Similarly, the US prime-time soaps popular through the 1980s and 1990s, such as *Dallas*, *Dynasty*, *Melrose Place*, and *ER*, are not expected by producers and audiences to continue indefinitely.

One direct byproduct of this defining feature of soaps is that the genre's writers have to maintain consistency with past stories; new tales must be in keeping with existing characters and their lengthy histories. This is far from easy. Donna Swajesky, a former head writer at *AW*, says of the practical difficulty:

> Everything's been done on a soap. I keep saying, well, what about this with Rachel? And they say, oh, she was blind three times, this happened, that happened. It's amazing to try to fill an hour a day for all these years. (Interview)

Writers must work fast to fill that hour daily, and as Jay Hammer, an actor who also writes soap scripts, told me, they draw on a variety of literary and dramatic sources for their story elements, including dramas such as those found in Euripides, Shakespeare, or Dickens, and in such melodramas as *The Perils of Pauline* (Interview). But while plot devices—love, betrayal, mistaken identity, inheritance, disinheritance—might be familiar from other dramatic forms, the way they are put together is wholly the property, indeed is the hallmark, of soap opera.[3]

The unending nature of soaps is decried by adherents to classical Aristotelian dramatic structure, which requires unity of action and closure. By that standard, and the standard of unity of time and place demanded by French classical dramatists such as Racine and Corneille, dramatic action has a beginning, a middle, and an end. A problem is posed, explored, and resolved; catharsis is achieved. Even prime-time TV sitcoms and dramatic series usually rely, whether well or badly, on this form. By contrast, continuing serials are "all middle, like life is" (Hammer, interview).

Soaps further contravene traditional dramatic standards by allowing many different actions and stories to occur at the same time. In this multiplicity, as well as in their unendingness, soaps may be seen as replicating real life in which many events occur simultaneously, and resolution of one problem may well create or be replaced by another. In a strange way, soaps do employ the Aristotelian dramatic structure, for embedded in the multiple sub-plots is a continual renewal of the familiar. The beginning of each story contains the seeds of its end, the resolution; but resolution of one story contains the seeds of the next. Over and over, we return to the same characters and community history, allowing an unending interweaving of new plot lines.

Here, then, is another crucial aspect of the soaps: in the twists and turns of their unendingness, soaps can be seen as reflecting the contours and texture of our own lives. We do not know when tragedy or happiness may occur in the lives of soaps characters any more than we do in our own lives.

We can predict and hope for a certain outcome, but we never really know the future in soaps, as in life.

Many analysts, especially those with a feminist perspective, see the unending, multiplex, and fragmented narratives of soap opera as an essentially feminine form of narrative (see Modleski 1982, Nochimson 1992, Williams 1992). The repetitive and continuing nature of soaps as compared to the Aristotelian ("male") narrative of problem, examination, catharsis, and resolution can perhaps be seen as an interesting parallel to the anthropological understanding of division of labour in most hunter-gatherer societies. In general, in such societies, women do most of the gathering of plant foodstuffs, grains, and small game. It is their effort that provides the dietary mainstays, and their labour that feeds their families and nurtures the children, thereby ensuring the continued existence of the group. However, theirs is not glamorous or exciting work, and it never ends. The men, the hunters, start their "narrative" by preparing their equipment and themselves for the hunt; they then seek out their prey, large game animals, and, in a happy ending, bring home the prized delicacy of meat. Although they will repeat their narrative, the end of each hunting expedition brings closure to the individual "saga." The labour of gathering, by contrast, simply continues day after day without high drama or closure. This less dramatic labour generates no cultural heroes, for while hunters of superior ability can be crucially important to group survival and composition, most, if not all, women can gather well enough. In television, especially North American television,[4] soap operas can be seen perhaps as analogous to women's role as gatherers: they are the continuing, undervalued efforts of storytelling which underlie network financing. Prime-time shows, which traditionally follow classic dramatic formulations, emulate the hunting role in that they receive the attention—the accolades or criticism—of society and the arbiters of dramatic value. And, like hunting, they usually present one or two "stars," whereas soaps typically involve a more egalitarian casting profile: they are the most ensemble of "ensemble shows" (Butler 1995).

This line of thought may indicate another element in the popularity of soaps: their elevation of the "mundane." Even granting the humble status just proposed, soaps are nonetheless fictions presented via the "glamorous" yet removed medium of television. They transpose the structure of everyday life to that electronic canvas and, in so doing, magnify it, vindicating the "ordinariness" of everyday lives.

These are the quintessential features shared by soaps on both sides of the Atlantic. But British and American soaps have their share of differences. The first contrast to draw between them is in their origins: American radio serials were made for commercial reasons, British ones for educational purposes. American serials were owned by cleaning product manufacturers, whose laundry soaps were the product of choice for the advertising segments—hence the tag "soap operas." (The industries in the US and Britain long resisted that term, and there still is considerable resistance to it in the UK.) The pioneering British radio serial *The Archers* was, by contrast, sponsored by the Department of Agriculture and was directed to men just as much as to women: it conveyed information about new agriculture technology through stories of a farming family. The stories of American serials, then, were essentially ways of keeping listeners tuned in for the commercials, and those of the British were intended to hold audience attention during a disguised lecture on farming methods.[5]

Whether for educational or commercial reasons, however, the extended narratives of soap opera have held radio and television audiences rapt for decades. And such long-term audiences have been beneficial for sponsors and networks, for rarely do ratings slip low enough for long enough that the show becomes unattractive to advertisers; soaps thus are not often cancelled. In addition, they are relatively low-cost productions, especially in the US, and traditionally have generated large advertising revenues:

> Because the soap operas generate steady profits (as a result of their continuous showings), they are far more valuable to the networks than the prime-time series.... More of the daytime revenue is clear profit ... because daytime programming is so much cheaper to produce. A half-hour prime-time show can cost $350,000. For the same money (or less), a full week of hour-long soap episodes can be produced. (Cantor & Pingree 1983: 54-55)

These figures, though much higher today, give us some idea of the ratio of daytime to prime-time programming costs. Further revenues are generated by sales of soaps around the world. For most nations, it is cheaper to purchase an existing soap than to produce their own, indigenous variety, and the networks and production companies profit by these international sales (Allan 1995: 12-13).[6] It is, however, becoming increasingly common for radio and television companies in other nations, such as Canada, to make soaps featuring local scenes and actors for either entertainment or educational purposes.

If soaps are extremely profitable for networks and sponsors and are watched by millions of loyal fans around the world, why are they still disparaged in the US by the television and acting industries? And they are; as one actor told *Soap Opera Digest,* "My agents have suggested taking soaps off my résumé. It's meaningless. It's like telling a Broadway producer how many high-school productions you were in. As unfair as that sounds, that's what it is. They won't look at it" (*SOD* Aug 2 94: 64).

The fans are disparaged right along with the actors. The stereo-typical image of a soap watcher is, as a fan put it to me, "fat, lazy house-wives who don't take care of their children." Although women still comprise the majority of soap viewers, and are more willing than men to acknowledge watching, many preface their comments on soaps with such phrases as "they're really stupid" or "I don't know why I watch, but..." Men are more reluctant to admit to being hooked on a soap. In one of my anthropology courses, for instance, of those students who admitted to watching soaps only one was male; yet in discussion with me after class, male students were as well informed about the plots as were the females. Still, the men did not watch, they said; their mother did, or an aunt, or their girlfriend.

Part of this male reluctance to admit to watching American soaps may be a reaction to the focus of the stories. In addition to endlessness, continuing serials are defined by their primary concern with domestic life and matters of the heart, both traditionally women's interests. Women are the official audience of soaps, according to the networks and judging by advertising focus. Here again, American and British serials part ways: British serials are directed more to men and families in general in their prime-time slots and in their storylines, which are less focused on romance than those of American serials.

Soap opera has also been slighted by mainstream media commentators willing to devote column space to critiques of sitcoms and any other type of television programming except the one most consistently watched by vast numbers of viewers:

> With a few notable exceptions, the television critic writing in maga-zines and newspapers has shown about as much interest in writing about soap operas as the restaurant critic has in writing about McDonald's—and for much the same reason: they are both regarded as junk. (Allen 1995: 5)

We can perhaps turn this observation on its head. Junk food is, after all, sometimes seen as fun food, familiar, even comfort food. And junk-food outlets are convenient places for families to gather and draw nourishment when Mom is too busy to set out the full-scale event within the home, or needs "a break today," allowing others to serve and clean up in a society where servants are not an option for most. Fast-food outlets are available to us all the time, at low cost, and perhaps their function is not so obviously to be sneered at. We might say much the same about soaps, in their presenta-tion of lives we wish we had, we're glad we don't have, or of which we have some second-hand experience. Perhaps both fast-food outlets and soaps are familiar, comforting asides to the frazzling pace of late-twentieth-century life.

In their neglect of soaps, television critics form an unlikely alliance with academic analysts of popular culture, who, with some exceptions, have also ignored or belittled their social influence. Soaps have been singled out as deserving of contempt, if not beneath it, for their quality, their time slot, their type of story, or their audience. Tania Modleski, writing in 1982, believes that soaps, as well as romance novels, are passed over for serious study because they are a *women's* genre, and therefore critical interest glides over them to fasten upon

> the aggrandized titles of certain class studies of popular male genres ("The Gangster as Tragic Hero") ... As Virginia Woolf observed some time ago, "Speaking crudely, football and sport are 'important'; the worship of fashion, the buying of clothes 'trivial.'" (Modleski 1982: 11)

Certainly, if one stacked the pages of analysis of the creative opus of soap writer Irna Phillips beside those devoted to the detective novels of Dashiell Hammett, the former would be dwarfed. But since the days of radio a critical literature on soaps has existed and over the past two decades has increased exponentially. The academic literature on soap opera is now as extensive as the stories are endless.[7] Within this specialized critical enclave, soaps and their viewers have been studied to a dizzying degree. The byzantine complexity of some analyses and what they claim to see in the stories inclines me to sympathize with the sentiments of Tony Warren, creator of *CS*: that soaps are simply "disposable entertainment," quickly made and quickly forgotten (interview). There is certainly a danger of over-analysis. But if the soaps do tell the stories of our lives and incorporate the fables and tales of our childhood and our society, this is equally clearly enough to make them worth a closer look.

It is tempting, in books like this one, to ask the big, ambitious questions such as: What role do soaps play in our lives? What is their "meaning"? In this case as in many others, the answers sometimes seem dismayingly out of proportion to the questions. The meaning that soap fans derive from the shows varies with the circumstances of viewing. Soaps can be company for those who live alone, temporary diversion during an illness, or material for innocent gossip with friends. Unlike real people, soap characters can be picked up and put down at will, and gossip about their doings will harm no-one. Through the soaps, we can become involved with the lives of people who demand nothing in return. Here an analogy with comfort food becomes persuasive: "[People] remember [*CS*] as something warm, something friendly and something familiar, and they return to it" (Warren, interview).

Soaps speak to emotions and situations known to all of us—love, pain, family relationships—whether or not their external worlds are familiar. You don't need to have visited Manchester to appreciate *CS*, nor do you need to know where Port Charles supposedly is located to enjoy *GH*. But as you are drawn into these dramas, you receive reflections of the concerns and aspirations of, respectively, British or American society.

I have long wished there was a soap that spoke to me as a Canadian, something that looked like my world. There have been a few short-lived attempts over the years. *The Plouffe Family* was a very popular radio serial in the 1950s; *High Hopes* was a short-lived but well-received television serial in 1978. CBC entered the soaps field in 1997 with *Riverdale*, set and made in Toronto. *Riverdale*'s Toronto, unfortunately, doesn't "feel" like the Toronto I know, so it doesn't really reflect Toronto for me, and certainly doesn't reflect the world I live in, in Newfoundland. In fact, the impression most people I know form of *Riverdale* is that it does not portray Canadian life. It is "too American" for viewers of *CS*, too "boring" for those who watch the US soaps. One might consider whether these responses reflect the English-Canadian national identity as often perceived by ourselves and others: influenced by the US, but nicer and therefore a bit dull. Unintentionally, such programmes mirror the Canadian cultural uncertainty of identity.

Hometown viewers may also be the harshest critics because of their familiarity with the place and the way of life protrayed in the shows. *CS* writer Tom Eliot said that he and his Mancester friends were quick to spot, and disapprove of, any inaccuracy in detail of Mancunian life in the early episodes (interview). And I, like most Canadian viewers, enjoy playing "spot the error" in Canadian productions, especially those aimed at a US market.

Like probably everyone who watches the soaps, I know the one I would make. It would follow the British model, localized and identifiable, yet speaking to universals. British serials successfully export their regionalized visions of their second and third cities around the world. Perhaps we should take this as encouragement; perhaps emulation of pan-American homogeneity in our case is also unnecessary. Canadian broadcasters are slowly taking more chances on regionally set, well-produced prime-time series, such as *North of 60* and *Black Harbour*. If the recent forays into soaps and regionally set and produced series auger well, maybe we'll see regional soaps for national broadcast yet.

"Will Faye Find Love?"

Because American producers essentially established the form of the soap opera, I will focus here on the development of radio and television soaps in the US,[8] with some brief comments on the British model for comparative flavour.

Throughout the 1930s and 1940s, American women and their families followed daily fifteen-minute episodes of domestic drama on their radios. *Ma Perkins, The Romance of Helen Trent, Just Plain Bill,* and *The Guiding Light* were among the longest running of dozens of American serials.[9] Many were introduced and punctuated with melodramatic interludes of organ music. The authoritative male voice of an announcer updated the story and posed tantalizing questions before each commercial break and at the episode's end: "Will Faye find love with the dashing doctor? Tune in tomorrow to *The Guiding Light.*"

The earliest US soaps functioned as filler programming for low-audience periods such as mid-day, when traditionally only housewives, pre-school children, and retirees were at home. Beginning on radio in the 1930s, soaps provided radio networks with revenue from companies like Procter and Gamble who bought blocks of airtime in those low-listening daytime hours (see Cantor & Pingree 1983: 31–46). The stories of family and women's lives that advertising agencies created for the sponsors caught listeners' interest and provided a regular audience for advertisements for the sponsor's products at bargain-basement costs. Hence, as we have noted, evolved the derogatory tag "soap opera," from the products the shows' sponsors marketed: cleaning products and laundry soaps.[10]

Some analysts have thought it significant that, as the ads tout ways of removing physical dirt (a traditional task of women), the series' plots are propelled by "dirty" little secrets and gossip (Allen 1995: 4; Baldwin 1995; Buckingham 1987). The term "opera" may have been added because of the throbbing organ music that interrupted radio soaps (see Silverman *et al* 1983) and because of the storylines' elements of melodrama with their focus on heartbreak and dastardly deeds. To some, this coupling of the elevated and the base signals a "travesty": "the highest of dramatic forms is made to describe the lowest" (Allen 1995: 4).[11] But a quick survey of opera libretti shows that the stories told therein deal with precisely the same topics as soap operas: love, murder, betrayal, deception.

These early serials conveyed messages about morality and how to deal with life and relationships: virtue was rewarded, and bad or deceitful characters eventually got their come-uppance. In some soaps, the social and moral messages were implicit in the story outcome; in others, the "voice of wisdom" character—Ma of *Ma Perkins* for example—would include a little homily on the value of honesty and loyalty at some point in most episodes. The ads sent another, more covert message. Simply put, sponsors hoped that audience members who cared about the characters would associate the advertised products with those characters and buy those brands rather than others. In suggesting that buying a particular soap brand would make domestic life more cheery or that "whiter than white" lingerie would revive the romance of a couple's early courtship, the ads shared some of the focus of the soap storylines: the perceived desire of women for romance and family life.

Although men and women populated the radio serials in roughly equal numbers, the characterization of the latter, who also comprised the target audience, was most crucial to the stories.[12] But analysts varied in their "readings" of the women in radio serials. For example, here is James Thurber's view:

> Commenting on ... Arnheim's (1944) scheme for classifying the people of Soapland according to three moral types—the Good, the Bad, and the Weak—Thurber points out that soap operas' Good Women were in the majority.... The Good Women of Soapland were strong in character, long-suffering, and unfailingly capable. But because the housewife audience insisted that women characters grapple with problems similar to their own, soap opera's women emerged as the "ideal" woman: the most put upon, most noble, most righteous, and hence most dehumanized creature ever to grace the air waves. (Cassata 1983: 88)

Another analyst, by contrast, viewed most radio soaps as falling thematically into one of three categories: "The Woman Alone," "The Problems of Marriage," or "The Family Saga" (Cantor & Pingree 1983: 21). In all three, however, women were portrayed as strong. Ma Perkins kept her family on the right track with her wise counsel; Mary Noble of *Backstage Wife* repeatedly proved herself more competent than her actor husband Larry; and lawyer Portia Manning of *Portia Faces Life* and Helen Trent of *The Romance of Helen Trent* might get themselves into romantic or career hot water, but they did not rely on a man to get them out of it (see Williams 1992: 17–18).

Of these three themes, the Woman Alone stories are especially striking in the message they conveyed to women: that a woman could be successful in a career and still be attractive to men. In the introduction to *The Romance of Helen Trent*, the announcer asked if a woman over 35—that is, a woman firmly established in some vocation and well able to earn her own livelihood—can find romance? The entire series was predicated on an affirmative answer. But Trent does not marry any of her suitors; she does not want to give up her career as a fashion designer. This suggests that it is career and *marriage* that are incompatible; at the time they were indeed thought to be mutually exclusive.

In fact, the careers of the women in the Woman Alone soaps were unrepresentative of women's circumscribed options in the society of the time, a society in which "there were few women lawyers in real life, and Helen Trent was probably modelled on someone very rare, the glamorous Hollywood costume designer Edith Head" (Williams 1992: 17). Here we see a paradoxical hallmark of American serials: their combination of fantasy with aspects of daily life. The series gave their target audience stories in which housewives could imagine themselves as important career women or being courted ardently by dashing young men. But they also validated their real lives by stressing the importance of homemakers as the foundation of the family. There is an intrinsic tension in soaps between the value of "ordinary" life and escapism in fantasies of glamour.

A V-E (Victory in Europe) Day episode on May 8, 1945, provides another take on the women in Woman Alone soaps:

> The Voice (male, of course) introduces "*Portia Faces Life*, a story reflecting the courage, spirit, and integrity of American women everywhere." (Well, maybe those soaps did have a feminist influence.) (Williams 1992: 18–19)

The influence may have been feminist, but these stirring words seem more likely, given the times, to have been grounded in a pragmatic manipulation of the feminine image when women's work was needed to keep families, and the US, functioning. During the Depression, women's ability to feed their families and, later, in the war years, to do "men's work" in factories and farms meant personal and national survival at times when men had few work prospects or were in the armed forces.[13] To extend the hunting and gathering analogy I outlined in chapter one, if natural or human-made disasters wipe out the game that men hunt, there are always some roots or berries women can gather to keep body and soul together.

During the Second World War, the predominance of women and women's work became more apparent. The absent (but alive) soldier was the actor in the national drama upon whom patriotic and romantic hopes for a happy ending were pinned. As in war, so in the soaps:

> The romance of it all is what we remember: I *longed* for Walter to return to Portia from Nazi Germany; and Leslie Raddatz quotes Thurber with scorn: "The chill Miss [Helen] Trent has had her men frustrated to a point [at] which a mortal male would smack her little

mouth, so smooth, so firm, so free of nicotine, alcohol and emotion." Says Raddatz, "That's the way James Thurber saw it. Not I." She recalls Helen's reunions with Gil Whitney, and what she imagined was not emasculation.... "Do you suppose that Gil came back just to hold hands? Not likely, say I." (Williams 1992: 18; emphasis in original)

But the sunny skies of peace did return, and with them another shift in what women were expected to do and be.

Rosie the Riveter Hangs up Her Overalls

The personification of American womanhood in wartime was Rosie the Riveter. In ads and posters her smiling, overall-clad figure, rivet gun firmly in hand, exhorted women to aid the war effort by working in factories, driving trucks, or doing any job that furthered the good of the nation. After the war Rosie made an abrupt exit; her place as icon of American womanhood in the 1950s was taken by a smiling Betty Crocker, who wore a frilly apron and held a wooden spoon. Betty Crocker smiled because she was happy spending her day at home thinking up taste delights for husband and children. This shift in symbols signalled the contraction of the female sphere: henceforth a woman's place was back in the home.

Women's return to the domestic realm had several benefits from the point of view of men and society in general. First, women concerned exclusively with homemaking were less threatening to men, especially men traumatized by war, than women working with heavy machinery. If Thurber was at all representative in his belief that soaps, and by extension society, had emasculated men, perhaps men wished to reassert their control. But whether they returned as heroes or as walking wounded, men wanted the jobs that the war economy had created, and they wanted a sense of power. In short, they wanted the jobs that women were filling. No government could welcome the prospect of the unhappiness of a large number of trained fighting men, accustomed to a military paycheque and well acquainted with the bitterness of unemployment in the years preceding the war, coming home to find their jobs taken by women. So women were again encouraged to do their patriotic duty: this time to leave the workforce to free up jobs for veterans.

The prosperity of post-war North America meant that many men, especially those in the middle class, could afford to support their wives and families on a single income. This came to provide a measure of social standing: because his "little woman" did not have to go out to work, a husband was seen to be successful. But women, now asked to fill their days with housework instead of factory work, needed to find meaning in that activity. At the same time, new appliances had eliminated much of the drudgery of basic domestic maintenance, and another "time-saver," precooked and packaged meals, was being aggressively marketed:

> By the mid-1940s, the American food industry had a single overriding ambition: to create a mass market for the processed food that had been developed originally to feed the armed forces. The technology for freezing and drying food, ensuring a long shelf life and general indestructibility, was available; whether or not it extended any real benefits to consumers who didn't have to dine in foxholes was immaterial. All that remained for manufacturers to figure out was how to convince the post-war American woman that she needed canned hamburgers and frozen Welsh rarebit (to name two of the earliest technical triumphs). (Shapiro 1995: 155)

And convince they did, ironically by telling women they were too busy to slave over the stove.

But busy doing what? In this post-war mythology, women could not be occupied with paid employment. And so, with few exceptions, 1950s advertising campaigns depicted women as

> frantic creatures racing from bridge parties to parent-teacher meetings to shopping sprees—an image that kept clear the distinction between earning money, seen as man's responsibility, and spending it, woman's greatest glory. Indeed, many authorities went quite far out of their way to avoid mentioning paid work when they conjured the typical daily challenges faced by wives. "Emergency meals are inevitable," counselled *Redbook* in 1956. "Whether they're caused by unexpected company, an over-busy day or something as drastic as a hurricane, be prepared with stored meals on your pantry shelf or in your food freezer." (Shapiro 1995: 156)

Magazines cautioned women about their responsibilities in the home, as did the communications of government, industry, and educators. What is important is the symbiotic relationship between soaps and society in which the stories were influenced by shifts within the culture and in turn reinforced those shifts.

Helen Trent Is Retired

A second major post-war influence on soaps was the advent of television. As they moved to the new medium, they carried the new agenda of domestication with them:

> Analysis of the radio soaps and of *The Guiding Light* scripts over 35 years indicate that ... the Woman Alone theme in radio, where women were portrayed as doctors, lawyers, radio announcers, actors, and businesswomen, may have been superseded by the [theme of the] traditional housewife in the 1950s and 1960s as part of the general feminine mystique that followed World War II. (Cantor & Pingree 1983: 149, citing Friedan 1963)[14]

According to Cantor and Pingree, "the one known Woman Alone story for television, *Miss Susan*, was introduced in 1951 and lasted only a short time" (1983: 22). Family sagas, which better suited the new ideology of woman's-place-is-in-the-home, became the staple storyline on television.

However, producers of early TV soaps did not simply act as agents of a new socio-economic blueprint for female roles. Changes in format and presentation style were also dictated by the nature of the new medium itself. For example, radio soaps, like novels, could whisk their characters to anywhere in (or out of) the world, as long as viewers' imaginations were nimble enough to construct such a place in the mind. These far-flung destinations could not easily be translated to the screen.

> A new kind of soap was needed: something more visual, with less talk and more action, yet realistic. Sandstorms in the Sahara [as in *Stella Dallas*] could be created by the theatre in the mind, but not by early TV budgets.... The fact that the visual medium was more lifelike also called for something closer to real time. Helen Trent, for example, could not be "over thirty-five" for twenty-seven years. (Williams 1983: 21)

Stories could now be *shown* as well as spoken, allowing more ways and thus, to some extent, greater freedom in their telling. However, *seeing* characters and localities also forced a greater realism in their aging and changing with time. As a result, the stories became more domestic and less fanciful than many of the radio serials. Given budget limitations, domestic life was easier to present visually and permitted a larger tapestry of characters and inter-relationships with a smaller number of stable characters and sets. TV soaps could "incorporat[e] the problems of marriage and mate selection within a larger [context]. Visual stories made a greater number of plotlines easier to develop.... Television soap operas usually revolve around the relationships of two families and their associates" (Cantor & Pingree 1983: 22). This made the development of a greater number of core characters and overlapping narratives feasible with a limited budget for sets.

The new medium also had to take account of the fact that viewers wanted to watch as well as listen. That either made it difficult to simultaneously perform household tasks or forced viewers to miss whole segments of the narrative (Cantor & Pingree 1983: 47; Williams 1992: 21).[15] So new methods of recapping information were introduced and are still used. If you miss a crucial visual scene while feeding the cat, it will likely be repeated in a memory flashback or as a recap, parts of key scenes replayed preceding or during the next episode. Events will be later discussed by characters in a way that can become boringly repetitive to regular viewers but, crucially, allows those who miss episodes or scenes to catch up. Recapping, explanation, and prediction on radio was done by the narrator; on television, these could be done through dialogue and visuals, making the announcer unnecessary.

Early 1950s television also ran many adaptations of radio soaps, but few of these survived more than a few years, with some notable exceptions: *Search for Tomorrow* and *Love of Life* aired for some 35 years after their start in 1951, and *GL* is still on the air after over 60 combined years on radio and television.

The Soaps' Progress

Soaps thrived in the US during the 1960s. Many that were introduced in that decade are still on the air: *GH, AW,*[16] *Days Of Our Lives, One Life To Live.* The so-called sexual revolution of the 1960s and a move to videotape were the major influences on the content and style of these soaps.

The early soaps were quite puritanical. Al Rosenberg of *Daytime Television* magazine recalls:

> [M]arried couples didn't sleep in the same bed together, they were always in twin beds. And there was a ... rule that whenever there was a romantic scene, or a love scene if you will, on a bed or a couch, one foot had to be on the floor. I don't understand the significance of that, but I remember that one foot—the actor who was on the bottom, I think, had to have a foot on the floor. (Interview)

They also continued to be situated in and focused on the life of the home:

> Day-time dramas originally were very slow-moving stories, kind of episodic. Basically they were about families, one or two families in a

neighbourhood. Two women would sit at a table ... and gossip about things that were happening in the neighbourhood. (Rosenberg, interview)

In interviews, both Al Rosenberg of *Daytime TV* and Tony Warren of *CS* laughingly recalled lengthy shots of acres and acres of floral carpeting.

Because they were shot live, early television soaps were simplicity itself. With rehearsal time as limited as it remains today, actors, in essence, were working in live theatre. Any slips in action and dialogue were seen by the audience; hence the need for austerity in scene structure, which made live production more manageable. Time constraints also played a role: carrying on the radio tradition of short episodes, the fifteen-minute and even half-hour soaps suited the live and then live-to-tape production. There could be artistic reasons as well. Most of *As The World Turns* was produced live until the mid-1970s because its creator, Irna Phillips, liked the immediacy and edge it gave the acting (Cantor & Pingree 1983: 60).

As well as having simpler storylines than today's soaps, the early TV soaps were less complex in appearance. Budgets were low, so sets were flimsy, simple, and few in number. From those humble beginnings it is possible, and revealing, to trace the evolution of the soaps' "look," the trends followed in soap opera sets and costumes: "Makeshift sets and dowdy attire have been replaced by stylish clothing, painstakingly careful set design, and a dramatic rise in the frequency of location shooting" (Neumann et al. 1983: 125). The authors of this assessment acknowledge the role budget constraints played in that evolution, but they see other factors as well:

Soap operas rely on representation rather than presentation set design. Sets are made familiar to the viewer not via intricate detail or elaborate design. They are, instead, marked by symbols, most of which reflect stereotypes recognizable to all audience members. Newcomb cites the example of the doctor's office, which need only be minimally represented, in order for the viewer to identify with it ...

[T]he most important aspect of the daytime serial is the individual face, in all its variety and with its vast capacity to express emotion. Soap opera sets may appear flimsy under scrutiny, but characters and their psyches are always substantive. (Neumann et al. 1983: 126, citing Newcomb 1974)

In other words, soaps prefer to exploit the rich resources of human expressiveness. Less vital aspects such as location are represented more schematically, more skeletally, and this is by design, not from poverty of resources or imagination.

By the 1970s sets of US soaps had become more substantial, but not necessarily more elegant or tasteful. Williams describes the sets of a soap in the
late 1970s as

> "homier"; in fact they are downright tacky. The *AMC* parlor of Tara
> and Phil Brent ... is a muddle of flowery wallpaper on a dark back-
> ground, lace drapes, a frou-frou china lamp, and an incongruous
> tufted leather "office" couch. A bedroom has stripes *and* flowers on
> the walls, and framed pictures even on the four door panels. (1992: 32)

In the late 1970s and 1980s sets became more tasteful and more expensive in appearance and production. One study credits the upgrading of soap
sets to a more "slick, expensive prime-time look" as a way of attracting and
keeping viewers accustomed to such production levels in their evening
viewing. Increasing budgets, of course, permitted more attention to be
devoted to set detail in order to give audiences what the *Young & Restless* set
designers call "visual excitement" in beautiful furnishings and homes.
"Visual excitement" is also created by greater use of location shooting,
either in nearby streets or in exotic foreign settings. These are possible only
because of increased budgets and the development of hand-held cameras,
which permit greater portability and therefore more flexibility in shooting
scenes (Neumann et al. 1983: 126, 128).

Stages of Soap Development in the US

The soaps of today bear little resemblance to the earliest ones, except in
their focus on stories of hearth and heart. One way of tracing their development, as we saw above, is to focus on such influences as broad changes in
the societies around them, prime-time television trends, and technological
development. We can gain further insight by tracing the evolution of soaps
through a typology of story "themes," or story emphasis. I will employ a
particular framework that sees television soaps as moving through six historical stages (Williams 1992: 26–32, following Gansberg 1988).

The first stage emphasizes "story" in advancing dramatic action as well as
providing a reason to dispense "moral advice."

Stage two focuses on "character," epitomized by the soaps of Irna
Phillips, who wanted to explore characterization over plotline. In 1956
Phillips broke new ground in *ATWT* by naming her characters, so audiences would more easily remember them. Before, characters were rarely
referred to by name as the emphasis was on the unfolding story rather than
on the characters involved in that story.

Stage three is the "psychological," best exemplified by Ted Corday and

Irna Phillips's 1965 *DOOL*. In this stage writers, with viewers, were not only getting to know the personalities of characters but delving into what motivated their actions. In the forefront of this trend was William Bell, creator of *Y&R* and *The Bold & The Beautiful,* who in 1967 was hired as *DOOL*'s head writer.

> He brought up the psychological aura and faded the traditional focus on characters like "Father" [Dr. Tom] Horton. Intensely emotional; based in deep, dark, even bizarre psychological states, usually sexual; Bell's stories were realistic only as fantasies—but that was the realism audiences wanted in the 1960s. (Williams 1992: 27–28)

The fourth stage, which also began in the late 1960s, is "social issues." It dates from the opening episodes of *Love Is a Many Splendored Thing*, an adaptation from a novel and movie, which ran from 1967 to 1973 and featured a romance between a Eurasian woman and a Caucasian man. That particular story, in its first year, was too hot for CBS and was dropped. But "issue" stories continued, from Bell, Phillips, and her protegée Agnes Nixon. Nixon had already written a story for *GL* in which the mother of the central family developed uterine cancer, at the time not thought to be a fit topic for broadcasting. The late 1960s saw the introduction of non-WASP lead actors, with Jewish, Polish, and black families taking centre stage. And social beliefs and experiences current in the late 1960s and 1970s were featured: feminism, abortion rights, the Vietnam War, drug use, child abuse. This new openness on serials extended, for the first time, to sex.

Young backburner[17] characters in *Love Is a Many Splendored Thing* signalled the move to the fifth stage: "kids." After network pressure caused the show to drop the central inter-racial romance story, it picked up a subplot involving young people, including Leslie Charleson (now Monica Quartermaine on *GH*) and moved it from the storyline backburner to the front. Bill Bell in his 1973 soap *Y&R* capitalized on youth, what Williams quotes as "'Bell's beautiful blondes' (male as well as female) [and] 'important' music (*Y&R*'s signature tune [which] became widely known as 'Nadia's Theme' after the Romanian gymnast Nadia Comaneci performed a routine to it in the 1976 Olympics)" (1992: 31). Kids and sex, troubled pasts and great but tormented loves, personal stories of sorrow and triumph, became a Bill Bell hallmark.

The sixth stage, "action," began in 1978 with what Williams calls the "Gloria Monty era" on *GH* (1992: 31) Kids, sex, *and* action/adventure (shot more often on location) took soaps and *GH*'s "supercouple," Luke and Laura, to mainstream media attention. The popularity of soaps became a topic of discussion in the media and in university courses, closet viewers admitted to watching, and plots became fast-paced and were often shot in exotic locations while characters were searching for or trying to evade villains (Williams 1992: 31–32).

Williams notes that 1980s prime-time soaps such as *Dallas* were instrumental in honing daytime soaps, influencing their more sophisticated look and stories. In tandem, evening and daytime soaps influenced prime-time drama series. The continuing and multiple-storyline form was quietly borrowed by shows such as *Hill Street Blues* and *St. Elsewhere* (1992: 32–33).[18] After a hiatus of a few years in the late 1980s after *Dynasty* and other such prime-time soaps ended, glamour and conniving returned to prime-time television in serials such as *Beverly Hills 90210* and *Melrose Place*. Soon after, continued narrative returned to popular dramatic series with such programs as *ER* and *Chicago Hope*. Teen-age prime-time soaps made a rebound in the late 1990s with shows like *Party of Five* and *Dawson's Creek* which have less glitz and less affluence among the characters, but just as much sex and angst as the veteran *Beverley Hills 90210*.

In the 1990s daytime soaps continued the trend towards action and adventure stories, including still more fantastic and drawn-out plotlines. The most extreme, perhaps, was the devil possession story in *DOOL*, which took up the better part of 1995. But the 1990s can be considered to mark a move to a seventh stage of soap development: the introduction of humour. In the past soaps rarely injected any humour into their characters or storylines and certainly did not engage in any self-mockery; that has changed. Lucy Coe went from *GH*'s 1980s villainess to being a genuinely funny character with her psychiatrist boyfriend as straight man. And Frisco Jones, also in *GH*, realized he had to look for a job when he found himself getting hooked on a soap.

Kale Browne, when he played Michael Hudson on *AW*, offered me this perspective on the historical lack of humour on American daytime TV:

> Americans have a terrible time making fun of themselves. There is no sense of humour about where they come from because it is so diversified.... The south is different from the north and northeast and California. There's jokes everywhere about every other part of the country.... In Canada it is very separatist in terms of nationalities. You've got strong French Canada, you've got English-speaking Canada, but then you've got every European community represented strongly. In the United States, it's been homogenized, but people still remember their roots and they're still a little defensive so there is no sense of humour at all. The English seem to be able to have a good laugh at themselves, we don't. That's why I think there is no humour in soaps. (Interview)

In other words, most Canadians and the British are familiar, maybe comfortable, enough with their differences to present them in dramatic form and even to laugh at them. The US is an uneasy coalescence of group identities, which the national ethos neither acknowledges nor accepts; the need to depict a united America crowds out the reality of cultural enclaves. These enclaves may not be admitted to "the American Dream"; they are nonetheless important enough that their representation is a delicate matter, hedged about with discomfort and taboos. Humour is too anarchic an element to introduce into this uncertain stability. This is gradually changing in the 1990s: WASP characters at least may now caricature themselves, though minority representatives remain earnest and steadfast, and are usually back-burnered.

The latter part of the 1990s has also seen another soap shift: to the vernacular in word choice. In a 1993 article entitled "What You'll Never See on My Shows!" CBS Director of Daytime Programs Judi Jenkins says:

> My little rule of thumb is that if you are calling someone a bastard, it better be because he does not know who his mother is!... My feeling is that it is not worth upsetting the audience over something that is not really going to change the sense of a scene.... Occasionally, we use a word that might have been questioned twenty years ago. [I think] that if you overuse it, it won't have any impact either. (*Daytime TV*, July 1993: 45–46)

Sponsors and networks assume the audience to be composed mainly of somewhat conservative middle- and working-class women who may be offended by coarse language, especially if their children watch with them. They do not want to offend audiences, so writers follow the old theatrical gauge of acceptability: Will it play in Peoria?

I have in recent years, however, heard characters called "bastard" and "bitch" (instead of the previous and still-employed "witch") with no implications regarding their parentage. On *All My Children*, Tad Martin told the destructively meddling Marion Colby that she was a "frustrated, malignant, old bitch." That set Marion back a bit; me as well. In context, it was the least that might be said. But after hearing such words used repeatedly over a few years, I have to agree with Jenkins that, if overused, their dramatic impact is lost.

The Street, the Community

In sharp contrast with the American experience, serials started on BBC radio as entertaining lessons. *The Archers* today more often discuss family matters or plan trips to France, but in the early days the family cheerfully absorbed information about cattle inoculation, new types of feed, and other such useful matters, which they discussed thoroughly for the benefit of listeners. British radio serials, like the early Canadian ones, were public service announcements in story form, as opposed to the American model of product advertisement in story form.

Early British television reflected what many consider a defining element of British society, its class structure:

> Down in London, at Gainsborough Studios—it's the old Lime Grove Studios ... —they used to make romantic comedies there, set in the seventeenth century. Lovely dresses and people swirling and swooping about. Up in Manchester, at the Dickenson Road Studios of Mancunian films, they made a series of funnies about Old Mother Riley—a music-hall character played by a man in drag called Arthur Lucan—and his beautiful daughter who worked in the laundry. That was the social divide ... working-class Britain lives in the north, speaks northern. (Crookes, interview)

The north was the site of humour, but was also the target of not always well-meant jokes by southerners. With its stereotype of northerners clad in Andy Capp-like cloth caps and clogs, the south of England regarded the north with the laughing derision reserved in Canada for "Newfies"; for itself it reserved the functions of "high culture." Low humour came from the north, "art" from the south. *CS*, the first continuing serial on British television, would turn that stereotype to its advantage by incorporating distinctly northern humour into the stories of northern daily life, including its economic poverty.

Ironically, continuing serials came to British television, as to American, for economic reasons, albeit for very different ones.[19] Until the late 1950s, the only television network in the UK was the state-operated public broadcasting system, the BBC. When legislation permitted private commercial broadcasting, regional networks, such as Granada Television in the twin cities of Manchester and Salford, were established. In order to avoid a deluge of American programming, legislators required broadcasters to incorporate a high percentage of British-made programs.

Unfortunately, making programs is costlier than purchasing already-existing ones. At the time, Harry Elton was a producer at Granada involved in developing cost-effective new and entertaining programming. A Canadian, he remembered American soap operas, which had already been running for several years in the US. More to the point, he remembered their phenomenal success. Since they use the same sets over and over and can hire actors on longer-term contracts, they are less expensive than limited-run series to produce. Here, then, was a way to satisfy the British programming requirements without bankrupting the studio. From these initial stirrings grew *CS*, Britain's first and still overwhelmingly popular continuing serial, whose genesis is discussed in detail in chapter three.

Conclusion

Soaps, then, have functioned as commercial and educational vehicles, sometimes combining the two. But whatever their origins, they tell stories that, through the years, still have at their heart the realm of the domestic and romantic. And these stories of heart and hearth, directed to women, have provided fertile ground for media analysts since the soaps began: what do these stories tell women about their real lives and their fantasy ones? In the following chapter I look at some of the theories spun in response to this question.

Two
The Theory of the Practice

The combination of a dissertation-in-progress on my desk and a baby or two in every other room of a small apartment forced me to desperate measures.... I turned on daytime television as an anodyne—with great reluctance, as I had always imagined soap opera in the demeaning terms in which it is conventionally discussed. Much to my surprise, though, I discovered that I liked the daytime serials. Once I became part of the daytime audience, it did not take me long to discover that my contempt for soap opera was an attitude I had adopted never having seen a soap opera, on the recommendation of social commentators who had also never really seen a soap opera ...

MARTHA NOCHIMSON,
ANALYST, FAN, AND WRITER, EDITOR, AND CONSULTANT
ON AMERICAN SOAPS (NOCHIMSON 1992: 1)

THE first tenet of fair criticism is to investigate—to *look at*—the subject of study. This might be thought too obvious to need stating. Yet, incredibly, many of the soaps's severest critics seem never to have deigned to look directly at what they presume to study. Or, if they do look, it is with apparent distaste and preconceived notions.

Critical analysis began soon after radio soaps first aired. At the request of American broadcasters, social scientist Paul Lazarsfeld formed a research team in the 1930s to inquire into who listened to the soaps and what messages they received (Williams 1992: 9). Thus began the history of research into the effects of soaps on their audience and the composition of that audience; the conclusions drawn were generally not favourable towards either. Not that soaps drew constant critical attention: such large-scale analytic interest as the Lazarsfeld effort would not recur until the feminist movement of the 1970s spilled over into university research. Ironically, most feminist researchers, though they saw soaps as the quintessentially female television genre, initially dismissed them or apologized for them; but more recent writers, such as Nochimson, are familiar enough with soaps to see the appeal and try to understand the stories and their audiences in their own context, without bias and without sneering. In general, analytic interest has risen and ebbed over the decades, but only in recent years have analysts been prepared to concede that any value whatsoever might reside in the stories.

This survey begins with the extreme negativity of the early analysts who saw nothing good in extended, domestic narratives. Typical of this period, though perhaps somewhat unorthodox in his methods, was a New York psychiatrist named Louis Berg who, in 1942, made news by claiming to have empirical evidence that radio serials produced all manner of psychological and physiological disorders in listeners (among them, gastrointestinal problems and nocturnal fright). He likened the followers of soap operas to "emotionally distorted" individuals who enjoyed lynchings and who "in the past had cheered on witch burnings" (Allen 1995:5, quoting Wylie 1943). Fortunately for the future of the genre and its audience, it was discovered that his data were gathered by monitoring only his own responses to the programs.

Another 1940s analyst, Rudolf Arnheim, adopted a quite different but no less biased tack, seeing the allure of radio soaps as grounded in base pandering to women's preferred image of themselves:

> They make the listener feel at home by offering her a world which outwardly resembles her own and in which people make themselves and others suffer by committing familiar mistakes and by displaying shortcomings of character. Although this presents to the listener a rather unvarnished portrait of herself, it cannot be expected to lead her to self-knowledge and self-criticism. Her identification is deflected to an ideal type of perfect, innocently suffering woman ... There is little effort to make the listener aware of her *prejudices and resentments*; rather she is carefully flattered. Men are shown to be inferior to women, the working class is ignored, learning is deprecated. (1979: 77–78)

In addition to cossetting housewives, Arnheim thought, radio soaps handed them an easy means of filling the void in their lives:

> [R]adio serials maintain a firm grip on so many millions of American women because they satisfy their psychological needs the easy way, by devices which are known from the psychiatric analysis of wish-dreams. The sociologist would have to tell us whether changing conditions have led children and husbands to live their lives so much

outside the home that it no longer offers the wife and mother enough scope for the expression of her capacities and affections.... Is the woman left behind as little more than a passive object of supply for the mechanism of production—a consumer, deprived of the creative talks to which her natural gifts and striving entitle her, left alone with a talking box as the only source of satisfaction? (1979: 79)

To his credit, Arnheim recognized the power of radio soaps in addressing women's lives. But his criticism of the stories and, by extension, their listeners—that soaps offered an easy escape from personal and societal problems, that producers did not present socially responsible answers to the problems they posed for their characters—seems high-minded to a fault. His analysis is an interesting harbinger of more recent criticism, particularly from feminist theorists who see soaps as encouraging female escapism. He most clearly anticipates this strain in the following passage:

Suitable adjustment to the problems of [a critical period] may be hampered where wish-fulfillment dreams are presented as reality: the middle-aged woman appears as youthful, attractive, ardently courted by desirable suitors. A reign of perfect justice, without any hint of how it is obtained, offers a gratuitous solution for problems of social life. (1979: 78–79)

Arnheim sees the avowed intention, acknowledged industry-wide, of providing pure fantasy entertainment as psychologically damaging: soap viewing allows the viewer to wallow in pure escapism rather than confronting real and often unpleasant social issues.

A 1950s commentator on American television programming neatly inverted Arnheim's view by suggesting that early television soaps, rather than providing "gratuitous solutions" to life's problems and thereby deflating them, instead exaggerate those problems. Marya Mannes saw soap plots as melodramatic histrionics, and, no stranger to dramatic form herself, she makes her point through a dialogue between two characters living in the year 2000 AD and discussing television in the 1950s:

Old man: There was, too, I remember, an extraordinary form of drama called the soap opera.... Many million women watched them every day, and wept.

Student: Wept? Why?

Old man: Because their troubles were slight compared to those of the characters, who lived from calamity to calamity; and they

wept from relief.... [G]ood women did housework all day
and drank coffee. All bad women had careers, flirted with
men and drank cocktails.... [B]ad men were usually culti-
vated, witty, and upper-class; and all the good men were
dull, faithful and humorless ...

Student: But were these people then reflections of living Americans?

Old man: In a sense, yes. Particularly in their manner of behavior, for
neither the young nor the old nor the good nor the bad
had any control over their emotions. I remember them as
chronic hysterics: storming, weeping, threatening, terrified
in situations requiring only a grain of common sense.
(1958: 102–3)

These brief excerpts are few and scattered, but they do provide the
flavour of the prevailing view in mid-century among those who cared to
concern themselves with soap opera. Communications and media study
remained a popular topic of analysis in the 1960s, but soaps did not spark
much critical interest: the focus was on mainstream programming, news, and
the shaping of understanding via the ever-increasing visual presentation of
information. Analysts such as Marshall McLuhan were interested in grasping
how the new medium of television shapes the form and presentation of its
own content, and how that changing content and the immediacy of image
alter social relations and our conception of ourselves and the world. Critical
theorists of the Frankfurt School, such as Jürgen Habermas, Theodor
Adorno, and Herbert Marcuse, were interested in the relationship between
reader (or viewer) and text (or screen) and the influence of mass media on
our understanding of our society and political structures. But they were also
interested in what was happening in "real" North American and European
culture in terms of student protests and the "counterculture." Soap operas
were but a tiny subsection of what was developing and changing in television and were swamped by the larger social dramas being played out in the
streets.

Soaps were rediscovered in academia in the 1970s and 1980s, partly
because the feminist movement and feminist scholarship revived interest in
women-oriented small-screen programming in the US and UK. By that
time, television soaps in both countries were well established, evolving in
production and message, and spreading to other nations. Although feminists
succeeded in focusing attention once again on the soaps, in this period they
had yet to exert decisive influence over the shape of the discourse. Feminist
theory simply had not yet developed the cultural profile, credentials, and
clout to speak loudly in the broad public forum of media studies. Centre

stage was instead taken by psychologists and communications analysts who conducted empirical analyses of story content and viewer response using psychological measures and quantitative methods. Journals were filled with articles itemizing the frequency and type of sexual references; the number of times alcoholic drinks figured in soap scenes and in what context; and the frequency of drug use or cigarette smoking, the types of characters involved, and the context.[20] Almost anything that could be itemized and counted, was.

There is of course no one simple explanation of this emphasis on the quantifiable in analysis;[21] but we can suggest some plausible reasons. The changes that the stories were undergoing at the time may have lent themselves to quantitative research methods. In the 1970s, as mentioned in the previous chapter, the soaps underwent a notable upheaval: they threw their puritanical code out the window. "Good women" still tended to their families, but the "bad women" got worse and had more fun. Bed-hopping increased, as did more explicit bedroom scenes. Controversial issues were raised, controversial behaviour engaged in. Such shifts and shocks to the sensibilities may have dismayed and daunted the onlooker of the time, however "professional" and "scientific," for the sensibilities of viewers in the 1970s were tender indeed in comparison with the hardened outlook of the 1990s. Earlier viewers may simply not have had enough exposure to become inured to the assault on previously sacrosanct codes of behaviour. Quite naturally, then, their first response was to whittle the shock down to digestible, quantifiable size: they counted indicators.

While the findings of these types of studies may be interesting, many of them are self-evident from casual viewing. I don't need to sit in front of my TV and count incidents in order to know that on American soaps more champagne and wine is consumed than beer or hard liquor. Also, with the exception of a few likeable renegade characters like *GH*'s Luke, only bad or severely troubled characters smoke cigarettes or cigars, and very few of those do. Charming facts these, but what do they mean? What do they tell us about the stories? Quantification analyses beyond a certain point are moot, for they focus on patterns of occurrence at the expense of the context, the larger picture, in which the measured elements occur. They can tell us little about that larger picture.

For instance, on American soaps a character lighting a cigarette or pouring a straight shot of liquor often signals that something bad is about to happen. That is the kind of contextualization that is easily missed by brute quantification unaccompanied by qualitative textual analysis. Quantification is also blind to the social message conveyed by the drinks of choice. Champagne and fine wines are expensive and are associated with the upper classes and wealthy, thereby adding to the aura of glamour and wealth in American soaps. The British serial *CS*, by contrast, has several characters who are regular smokers, but whose smoking never functions as a signal of situation or action to come. Bet Lynch was frequently seen with her trademark cigarette holder; other characters are seen smoking regularly, as smokers do, some even smoking after the birth of their children. Smoke drifts up from the hands of extras in the pub—all signifying nothing whatsoever except that these characters have a taste for nicotine. And the drinks requested at the Rover's are consistent with Britain's everyday drinking habits: a pint of bitter for the men, a half of lager, gin and tonic, or wine for the women. Context, or the social codes and expectations that govern particular situations, begins to seem crucial in decoding the messages of the soaps, and in clarifying their cross-cultural differences.

This is not to say that quantitative studies have no role whatsoever in understanding these shows. Statistical tabulation can give empirical evidence of trends in story type and in differences between shows, and can summarize information on why viewers watch and how they "read" the stories. In that way, they provide valuable information on the nature of soaps and their fans. But they should be buttressed by other types of analysis that further other levels of understanding of soaps and their audiences:

> The social scientist's "counts" (of scenes, etc.) should be made because there are surprises (*General Hospital*, e.g., known for its action, is number one in friendship scenes). [But] to know how the multiple stories of soap operas are put together, a structural analyst needs to go to the people who make them. And to know what they mean, a researcher must listen to the people who watch. (Williams 1992: 11)

Quantitative researchers do, of course, go to soap audiences, but most often only to itemize and statistically compare the range of responses to specific questions. One area of intense interest to quantitative researchers that illustrates the bluntness with which the instrument can be wielded is the question of how viewing television soaps influences viewers' perceptions of their society. A typical approach with this field of enquiry is known as "cultivation effect analysis." One of its main advocates, George Gerbner, theorizes that, in essence, you are what you watch. Television scenarios replace lived reality and "cultivate" perceptions of society. Viewers are the *tabula rasa* upon which soaps (and other television programs) inscribe behavioural and social attitudes and standards. Levels of violence, for instance, could correlate positively with the amount of television watched.

> Respondents [in Gerbner and Gross's 1976 study] were ... asked to estimate their chances of being involved in some sort of violence "during any given week." Here the "TV answer" was "1 in 10" while the "real world answer" was "1 in 100." Again, heavy viewers of tele-

vision, regardless of level of education, amount of newspaper reading, age or gender, were more likely to give the "TV answer" than would light viewers of television. (Carveth 1992: 4–5)

Carveth's own research findings on perceptions of societal levels of sexual promiscuity, based on a survey of college students who watched soap operas, failed to unearth any tidy correlation between perceptions of a "promiscuous world" with heavy and/or long-term viewers and a "non-promiscuous" world with non-viewers. Taking other factors into account, he suggests there may be some evidence of a slight cultivation effect.[22] But the degree to which television viewing influences perceptions of reality, he believes, may depend on the degree of familiarity people have with the matter at issue. He makes the sensible point that for such matters as "occupational portrayals" (percentage of the population employed, for instance, in law enforcement) and frequency of incidents of violence, television may be one's main source of information, but "the average person is likely to have significant direct experience in marital and sexual relationships" (1992: 15).

Television presentation of an issue, then, is less likely to influence one's perception of that issue if one has additional sources of information on it. Nonetheless it seems safe to say that entertainment programming, as Gerbner and others have demonstrated, can influence (though hardly dictate!) our perception of social realities. And it can do so in a myriad of complicated ways. We have so far considered only one manner in which messages are interpreted once they reach us; but many factors can influence the shape of the message that is sent in the first place. Long before it reaches us, that is, information can be molded through subtle processes: What information counts as information, as "news"? Who decides this? What are their criteria? Because television's influence on how we see our world is complex, so has analysis of it been.[23]

The best tack is a judicious perch on the fence: to respect both the power of the media to influence the ways we think, and the ability of humans to think for themselves: to weigh, judge, and reason critically and independently. This second factor, of human intelligence, is in short supply among soap fans according to much early as well as later quantitative analysis. This is not surprising, given that quantitative researchers seem to have felt antipathy for the soaps; they would naturally extend this sentiment to those who enjoyed such debased entertainment. "Few empiricists," according to one writer, "are [soap] fans.... The most troublesome characteristic of mass communications research is a pervasive, elitist assumption that the audience can be controlled" (Williams 1992: 10). Williams agrees with Robert Allan's (1985) assessment of many quantitative empirical studies of soaps:

"Fear" of soap opera influence comes largely from the [analysts'] belief that characters are real to viewers, he says, and "once again the complex relationship between soap operas and their viewers has been greatly oversimplified." (1992: 10)

For two reasons, soaps are particularly tricky for understanding the interplay between fiction and real life and the relationship of viewers to the stories they watch. First is the type of stories told, which are identifiable to some extent with viewers' lives and concerns. The second factor is those stories' longevity: soap fans may have "known" characters and families for most of their lives, and their relationship to their story and to other fans must be carefully teased out.

We can also issue a caution in the other direction: soap viewers incorporate the full spectrum of human credulity. Consider that Tony Warren, creator of *CS*, remembers people writing letters of application to Granada Television for Hilda Ogden's cleaning job in the Rovers Return when she quit work (Warren, interview). And stories abound in the American soap industry of actors being verbally or physically assaulted by irate viewers after their characters did something despicable. But that is part of the task of analysts: to explore and understand the full range of fans' reactions to their stories, recognizing that human perceptions and grasp of the "reality principle" vary as widely as any other human feature.

We are much more likely to do an adequate job of this, however, if we look at the soaps not from the dizzying heights of condescension, but from the perspective of an attentive viewer, observing critically but allowing engagement with the pleasures of soap viewing:

Perhaps this is the basic problem: finding scholars who will put in time watching soaps and who love the stories enough to gossip about them with other fans. (Williams 1992: 11–12)

There is a tension, admittedly, in the notion of a "scholarly fan": essentially it involves "witting seduction," a concept that seems to verge on the oxymoronic. But only seemingly; the two stances are not logically mutually exclusive. They simply require vigilance on the part of the onlooker, lest one orientation gain ascendence over the other.

Let us, then, return to the trail of analysis through the decades. Quantitative studies reached their zenith and then declined in proportion to ethnographic and structural "textual" studies of soaps, using such theoretical frameworks as semiotics, critical theory, and Marxism, among other literary and social analyses. In particular, a wholly different approach to the study of soaps developed in the 1970s: feminist analysis of the stories told, the women who watched, and how the stories influenced them. These feminist scholars were not, unfortunately, the "engaged viewer" so lacking among soap analysts. Like empiricists, most of the 1970s feminists seemed not to like soaps or the women who watched them. Their antipathy is not surprising, in that feminist thinkers of the 1960s and 1970s were struggling to redefine the boundaries of the "female" in both characteristics and behaviour. The female characters on the soaps, preoccupied with romance and family, presented the stereotypes feminists were trying to overcome.

So why did feminists so assiduously involve themselves in studying soaps, single-handedly fuelling the resurgence of interest in soap opera and television study from the late 1970s to the early 1980s? According to Brunsdon, the interest was "a combative [one], a commitment to knowing thine enemy" (1995: 58). Feminists wanted to understand the messages about women conveyed by soaps and their effects on viewers, the better to counter them. In particular, feminist analysts believed that the foundation of effective resistance was careful scrutiny and understanding of such stereotypical polarities as housewives and sex symbols (for instance, Marya Mannes: "good women who do housework and drink coffee" and "bad women who have careers, flirt, and drink cocktails" [1958: 102]).

This was the era of consciousness-raising, when small groups of women met regularly to discuss their innermost feelings and their social and political realities in order to improve their self-esteem and circumstances. This was also the heyday of such slogans as "the personal is political," which Brunsdon considers a factor in the choice of "soft" entertainment programming for feminist study (1995: 58–60). Soap operas are domestic, personal, about the minutiae of life (women's realm) rather than the outward and action-oriented world (men's realm). And so just as feminist historians explored the field of social history, the study of "ordinary" lives, feminist media analysts studied the ignored domestic dramas. Still, the content of soaps stuck in many a feminist craw; few could bring themselves to see much of value in the stories, which were often thought to be bad for women, and their viewers were not considered terribly bright:

> The feminists are not as bad as Muriel Cantor and Suzanne Pingree, who characterize the female audience as "intellectually limited, socially isolated, lonely and/or emotionally deprived." But the feminists can derogate: "The family is, for many women, their only support, and soap operas offer the assurance of its immortality.... As long as the children are unhappy, as long as things don't come to a satisfying conclusion, the mother will be needed as confidante and adviser, and her function will never end" [quoting Modleski 1932: 88, 90].
>
> At the least the feminists distance themselves from their subjects.... "We" are the ones who can understand; it is the "others" who watch [soaps]. (Williams 1992: 7–8)

An apt illustration of this distancing, of what I have called analysis from "the outside," is provided by Modleski, who concludes her essay on soap operas by saying:

> It is important to recognize that soap opera allays *real* anxieties, satisfies *real* needs and desires, even while it may distort them.... As feminists, we have a responsibility to devise ways of meeting these needs that are more creative, honest, and interesting than the ones mass culture has supplied. Otherwise, the search for tomorrow threatens to go on, endlessly. (1982: 108–9)

Modleski employs an "us/them" dichotomy, a not-so-subtle patronizing of soap fans as blinkered and benighted, in her call for a "better" vehicle to satisfy the itches soaps scratch. In this she joins the company of such fearmongers as Dr. Berg,[24] all of whom are terribly exercised about the damage soap viewing inflicts on poor hapless (read: witless) female viewers. Modleski differs only in that she patronizes from the perspective of "sisterhood." But at least she acknowledges that soaps do speak to women's lives.

To give Cantor and Pingree their due, the characterization of soap fans attributed to them by Williams is not theirs; in the portion so scathingly quoted they are summarizing previous analyses by other writers, and it is those analyses that regard soap fans as "intellectually limited" and so on. They review the conclusions of a 1980 study of soap audiences, then go on to question the validity of making generalizations:

> older women watch soap operas because they provide surrogate friends ... [and] home-oriented viewers watch because they are relatively cut off from adult companionship during the day.... No explanation is given to account for so much viewing among the youth category, but the fact that [these young people] have little interest in intellectual subject matters implies that [they] are more limited in resources than others. We are not denying that explanation, but because no one has fully investigated the various segments among soap opera viewers, we remain limited in the generalizations that we make. (Cantor and Pingree 1983:126, commenting on Frank and Greenberg 1980)

Ironically in view of Williams's reaction to their work, Cantor and Pingree in fact initiated a new direction in soap analysis: they acknowledged their enjoyment of soaps, thereby smoothing the way for other researchers to do likewise and for seeing appreciation of the stories and fans as an important part of analysis. Nor, unlike many early feminist analysts, do they see the stories as fantasy whitewashing of women's experiences and abilities.

And unlike many later feminist analysts, they do not celebrate it as a form of female resistance to the patriarchy. Here is how they playfully view their purpose:

> We learned that soap opera production is truly another world. History shows that as the world turns, so does its contents. As scholars, we will continue to spend the days of our lives in re-search for tomorrow ...
>
> Our purpose in writing this book is to integrate the soap operas into the field of mass communication. The soap opera is important as a form of popular culture and as an economic commodity, and in comparison to other kinds of television drama, it is unique. (1983: 10, 11)

Other researchers followed their lead. Some, like Nochimson, quoted at the beginning of this chapter, discovered that they themselves enjoyed the stories. Increasingly in the 1980s, writers admitted to appreciating the pleasures of an essentially female narrative. This marks a turning point in the critical understanding of soap opera, a division of approach into what we might call the "view from outside" versus the "view from inside." The former often subtly metamorphoses into "the view from above" with a critical distance so vast that perception blurs. The latter involves enjoyment of the medium of study without the loss of critical distance; the different angle of approach can lead to insights otherwise unattainable.

A fine example of the contrasting methods is found in the work of Nochimson and Haskell. In 1992 Martha Nochimson discussed a 1973 study by Molly Haskell of "women's films," romantic movies of the 1930s and 1940s. (Albeit not a study of soap opera, this work, in its analysis of central elements and even in its phrasing, is strikingly similar to those of early soap commentators.) She quotes Haskell,

> At the lowest level, as soap opera, the "woman's film" fills a masturbatory need; it is soft-core emotional porn for the frustrated housewife. The weepies are founded on a mock-Aristotelian and politically conservative aesthetic whereby women spectators are moved, not by pity and fear but by self-pity and tears, to accept, rather than reject, their lot. (1992: 22)

One can only wonder what Haskell makes of *real* soap opera. Nochimson compares Haskell's "purportedly feminist dismissal of daytime serial" to Dr. Berg's reaction to radio soaps, in so doing tracing a dangerous subtext:

Like Berg's "experiment," Haskell's conflation suggests a hysterical subtext. These hostile critics appear to react defensively against a narrative in which, as they perceive it, emotions are out of control, a narrative form that refuses to acquiesce in the conventional elevation of reason over emotion. (1992: 23)

In this refusal to place reason high above vulgar emotion we can see one way in which adopting the "view from inside" infuses theory. If the soaps do allow untrammelled emotion, and an analyst enjoys and gets caught up in the experience of viewing soaps, then the resulting analysis will take that enjoyment as data, to be questioned perhaps, but certainly *acknowledged*. This approach is unprecedented in that it considers emotion to be, in a word, *legitimate*.

Nochimson's reaction against such analysts as Haskell, then, is informed by a counterview that up-ends the allegedly traditional (male) belief in the primacy of reason over emotion. This view is based on feminist analyses that look at female forms of discourse and psychological development such as, most famously, Carol Gilligan's *In a Different Voice* (1982), discussed by Nochimson,

[Such] theories ... make it easier to imagine the integrity of soap opera narrative as a form of feminine discourse in which the energy of the protagonist comes from expressing feeling, not controlling it. (Nochimson 1992: 23)

Much of the analysis of the 1990s has placed soaps within the context of a feminine-based discursive narrative form—soaps as women's subversive narratives and female-directed storytelling—rather than the more widely accepted logically structured narrative, which is understood as masculine in its approach. The 1990s, in other words, saw a head-on collision of paradigms.

As analytic perspective and focus have expanded in this decade, so have the number of male and female writers willing to admit their liking of soaps. But adoption of a common vantage point—what I have called the view from inside—has certainly not resulted in uniformity of opinion. A few examples of the approaches taken by current feminist soap analysts gives an idea of the range of their views despite their common underpinnings.

Martha Nochimson (1992) looks at soaps in terms of Greek drama and psychological archetypes together with a semiotic study of camera shots. She sees her task as understanding soap opera as "a resistant feminine discourse." Against the backdrop of Hans-Georg Gadamer's exploration of individual realities versus "public Truth," she argues that "Hollywood fantasy is the fantasy of patriarchy. In soap opera, by contrast, another kind of yearning emerges, one rarely permitted expression in our culture. Soap opera includes a female subject" (1992: 1–2).

Carol Williams (1992) discusses soaps in relation to folktales, psychological and dramatic archetypes, and the structure of the writing and production form. She describes her purpose as the study of "myths," as an attempt

> to show soap opera as story, ancient act against chaos, stay against confusion ...
>
> Symbolic order. Ritual participation. Soap opera, then, is cultural, primal, and mythic. It is not brainwashing and can be therapeutic, as, for example, in the work of Anne Killguss, a psychiatric social worker who in 1971 came to soap opera accidentally because of a patient who would not talk ... "All I do is ... I watch my programs. Soap operas." Through talk about her stories with Killguss, the woman was led to talk about herself. (1992: 6)

Mary Ellen Brown compares soaps, as women's discourse, with the underground "ritual of reversal" aspects of "Carnival." Carnival is a time in which "unacceptable" social behaviour and role reversal in costumed parades signify a casting off of the usual social conventions and an "up yours" attitude towards them, as well as a way in which social subgroups constitute themselves by setting themselves apart from dominant powers.[25] She sees a striking parallel between women's subcultural "language," that of the soaps, and the "language" (structure, assumptions) of Carnival:

> The non-hierarchical juxtaposition of various stories in a soap opera, or of various subjects in women's gossip, can be described as a set of "motley moments," and the particoloured motley dress of the jester is emblematic of the capacity of contradictions to provoke a carnivalesque laughter. (1990: 183)

Brown and other recent feminist analysts who see the structure and content of soaps as a form of female narrative therefore consider it a kind of female power.[26] Brown takes her analysis in a fascinating new direction by discussing soaps in terms of their capacity to embody and validate women's talk and women's role in the dissemination of information. She reclaims "gossip" as a positive female practice; it is also, of course, what propels the narrative of soap opera:[27]

> *Gossip*, n. (*arch*): a woman friend who comes at a birth; a familiar friend; one who goes about telling and hearing news, or idle, malicious, and scandalous tales ...
>
> The woman friend or relative who, in the first definition, comes to

give comfort and spiritual support at times of crisis or transition ... is seen in the latter definition from outside the women's network as a threat, as the agent of a subversive and malicious information service. In contrast to the overwhelmingly negative characterisation of the talking and intimacy that are part of women's oral culture, there are many positive terms for men who speak publicly: bard, preacher, orator, or soothsayer ... soap opera fulfills many of the same functions, and attracts much the same sort of criticism, as the figure of the gossip in women's oral cultures. What is it then that is so threatening ...?

More than the content of such gossip, it is its aimless style that is apparently most objectionable. The Biblical admonition by St. Paul to ignore "fables and endless genealogies, which minister questions rather than godly edifying" (Timothy 1:4), suggests that it is the open-endedness of such talk ... Unmotivated talk that raises questions, explores possibilities, and continues for its own sake, for the joy of talk, implicitly denies that language is capable of embodying the one true word that is at the basis of official Christian dogma. (Brown 1990: 183–84)

The meaning of "gossip" has changed, but not the censure of those who indulge in it. Brown is right that women as disseminators of information have long been regarded as trivial, even dangerous. This taint of triviality also, of course, continues to cling to the soaps, and to underlie a certain amount of the things that are written about them. Many still cling to views of women's discourse (gossip, if you will) as petty, trivial, forgettable; their analyses of soaps are shot through with this presupposition.

Analysis and reality do not always coincide, and analysts do not always know the difference. A 1930 ethnography about the Ibo society of southern Nigeria, written by a man (Badsen 1938), described a social order where women had no property rights, working their husband's fields, but owning nothing except the produce they took to market, with their only power derived from their job as cook. If provoked, a woman refused to cook for her husband, thereby both embarrassing him and forcing him to fend for himself until he mollified her. Another account of Ibo women written by the wife of a British colonial administrator (Leith-Ross 1939) averred that the produce the women sold at market was the real basis of the economy. Travelling to markets throughout the region, they gathered and shared news. The information network in which they participated, and their husbands did not, as well as their control of their profits and product, gave them enormous *unofficial* social and political power. Their husbands and the colonial authorities assumed that women, and their market earnings, were insignificant, and this belief served the women well. It exempted their income (most of the total family income) from colonial taxation. It also allowed them room to "manoeuvre," that is, it gave them a certain power over their husbands and the colonial officials, power that they utilized any time they considered their freedom to be endangered. Patriarchal ideologies, both Ibo and British, unintentionally fitted, and served, Ibo women's cultural and social organization very nicely, despite surface appearances. Similarly, the surface triviality of soaps provides a forum for discussion of women's concerns that is largely ignored by arbiters of social relevancy.

Working-Class Culture and CS

British ethnographic, Marxist, and feminist studies of stories and audiences differ from American analyses in ways that reflect the different social landscapes. British serials have been shaped by a national ethos rooted in a highly specific understanding of social class, place of origin, and identity. The standard supra-cultural theoretical perspectives informing scholarly readings of serials have slightly different fodder to chew on in Britain, and it is crucial to grasp the nature of this difference.[28]

CS, the grand dame of British continuing serials and the bench-mark for all later ones, provides a convenient vehicle for generalized comments on these shows. In particular, one take on the show is insightful: Richard Dyer's (1981) comparison of that serial with an influential book published in 1957, *Uses of Literacy* by Richard Hoggart, specifically in its treatment of working-class society.

> What [Hoggart] set out to describe was the "common sense" of "everyday life" for the working class, in a way that both caught the apparent naturalness, down-to-earth, air-that-you-breathe feeling of such notions and yet acknowledged the specificity.of the actual content of common sense. (1981: 2)

According to Dyer, Hoggart's view of the working class marks a turning point in British cultural history (1981:2). Social-scientific study had until then emphasized economic and political relationships within British society as a whole; the life of working-class people outside their economic conditions and the role of labour in political structures was largely ignored. Hoggart differed from previous interpreters of working-class society by shifting the focus of critical attention from the society at large to an enclave within that larger society, the culture and social relations of working-class communities. In that way, says Dyer, his study was "anthropological." He was interested in the interaction of individuals within a community, and the "sets of assumptions [and] ways of getting along together" (1982: 2) rather than relations between that community and a larger social entity.

Here his project begins to show striking parallels with that of the creator of *CS*, Tony Warren, who envisaged a show about life in Lancashire: a "fascinating freemasonry, a volume of unwritten rules. These are the driving forces behind life in a working-class street in the north of England. The purpose...is to examine a community of this nature, and to entertain" (Nown 1985: 25). The working-class common sense of which Hoggart wrote is an analogue of those unwritten rules that Warren sees as lying at the heart of *CS*. Both concern the wisdom that consists in living harmoniously within a particular group with its own societal mores, as opposed to knowledge about the society outside that group or the ability to survive in its shadow. And both analogues, in Dyer's view, are infected by romanticism.

Dyer first criticizes what he calls Hoggart's "unqualified celebration" of working-class common sense for its "reconfirmation of a long-standing belief in the ebullient cornucopia of low-life existence" (1981: 3). In other words, it is a misty-focused, romanticized view of what can be a culture of desperation, with the health problems, domestic violence, and criminal activity associated with entrenched generational poverty. Dyer and other analysts chide *CS* for ignoring the same brutal facts, for rose-tinting working-class life.

Hoggart partly achieves this mystification of working-class culture, says Dyer, by omitting "all reference to the political and work institutions of the working class" (1981: 3), meaning that the central, defining feature of working people—paid labour —is absent from his analysis. In Hoggart's defence, Dyer notes, he did write at a time of higher wages, strong unions, and greater individual purchasing power. (Although the boom occurred later than in the US, the post-war years in the UK were also a time of economic growth, at least for some, making class membership a matter of cultural definition as much or more than of income level.) Dyer sees Hoggart's view of a depoliticized working class as leading him to unduly emphasize the role of "home and community ... and women" (1981: 3): in Hoggart's presentation women are strong, the moral centres of their home and community. But, again, he faults Hoggart for depoliticizing the gender relations of the workplace and home, where women's work may be undervalued monetarily and underappreciated in the household. In all, these themes of depoliticization and romanticism in tandem with Hoggart's hopes for the survival of this culture make his study "nostalgic," a sentimental and to some extent outdated image of working-class life. And, adds Dyer, "it is easy to see how [these elements also] ... inform *Coronation Street* and indeed come close to defining its fictional world" (1981: 4).[29] I will have more to say on nostalgia in British serials in chapter five; here, the analyses of Hoggart and Dyer are illuminating in understanding how British serials constitute a very different creature from American ones. The basic objects of analysis in Britain—class, community—are either absent from or given a wholly different spin within American society.

Myth and Reality in the Soaps

Soaps in the US and the UK have changed in look and stories over the decades, and so have analytic trends. Virtually all critical approaches are of potential value, since serials and their viewers are a very complex lot. As well, such trends ought to be evaluated partially within the terms of their social and intellectual era: what was written in the 1940s, for example, may have made sense given the assumptions of the time, even if it seems anachronistic now.

Still, the early, empirical soap analyses exhibit a shallow understanding of the "meaning" of soaps and an excessive concern with quantification. In the US and UK, early feminist analyses can be faulted for their focus on "woman as victim" or "woman as stereotype" in storyline and audience response analyses. And some of the newer textual critiques may go too far the other way, seeing too much in soaps. Perhaps the dramatic and psychological archetypes authors such as Williams and Nochimson see in the stories do exist in them, simply because they are universal elements of the human mind and therefore are found in all stories (see Levi-Strauss 1967; Propp 1968). But while parallels with classical archetypes may lurk in the subconscious of soap writers, time constraints alone make it doubtful that they are a driving force in the conscious creation of a story plot.

In the end we need to maintain a firm grasp of common sense: modern soaps are designed to entertain. Granted, they are rooted within specific social and political realities and created at a certain time in history in a particular place. The environment and ideologies within which they are written influence, indeed shape, the way the stories are told, and attention to these features will yield much valuable information. But it does not follow that soaps are intended to change the way people think.[30]

That said, of course the soaps appeal to familiar, common human situations, dilemmas, emotions. How could they not and still appeal to a broad swathe of humanity? Yet the human predicament is rich enough to constantly appear in new guises. Soap head writers Michael Malone and Craig Carlson know this:

> "There are only so many stories, and by now, they've all been told," Malone [says]. "They just haven't been told by the same writer." To illustrate, he mentions Cristian and Jessica's romance (*OLTL*). "The story of two young people who fall in love and cross a great chasm of class and race is not new. It's Romeo and Juliet. But because of who Jessica is and who Cristian is, it's not going to be like any other Romeo and Juliet story." (*SOD*, February 13, 1996: 46)

"You tend to tell your own story," Carlson explains. "It's like Charles Dickens, who tended to tell these stories of abandoned children over and over again in different ways.... I think soap writers are the same; we all have our own way of telling stories." (*SOD*, February 13, 1996: 48)

Soaps do present universal stories in the framework of their present-day societies. Many are so firmly entrenched in our minds—and the minds of soap writers—that they will inevitably be retold in the storylines: Cinderella, the frog who is really a prince, the Beast taught to love by Beauty. American soaps are peopled by characters from Mother Goose, but are set in modern-day America with some realistic portrayals of human emotions and relationships. It is this distance between fairy tale and social reality that brings American soaps in for criticism.

In British serials, Mother Goose does not have such a free hand in character and story development, but other archetypes of popular fiction are employed. Elsie Tanner and Bet Lynch over the decades of *CS*'s life have represented the "tarty" woman who attracts men like bees to honey, *à la* Shirley Maclaine's Irma La Douce. The young, shifty laddo has had several incarnations, as has the older, lay-about, married version. Stan Ogden, Jack Duckworth, and Les Battersby are some of the middle-aged men who, over the years, stymied their wives' efforts to be accepted as respectable. As Bill Tarmey (Jack Duckworth on *CS*) said to me, "I could take you to a pub that is the Rovers, a person who is Percy, who is Jack" (interview).[31]

Story themes, whether from Euripides, the Brothers Grimm, or Andy Capp, when used in stories set in "real"-looking environments cause analytic difficulties. Because of the layering of "reality" and fiction, messages both intended and unintended can get skewed. For the most part, viewers employ the long-standing dramatic-reading device of suspension of disbelief; whether or not what they view on TV matches their life experience, they know (for the most part) that it is only a story. We "know" that in "real-life" America few poor girls catch the eye of and marry a local millionaire, as we "know" those small working-class streets in England don't usually contain so many residents who've been married five or six times by the age of fifty. We're watching a *story*—we want to see the fairy tales and we want the excitement of romance and betrayal. The soaps give us the mundane: people doing the ironing and worrying about their kids' grades. They also give us romance and fantasy, the escape into unreality that we want. Soap viewers generally distinguish between the two levels of viewing, and the purposes of entertainment, in their understanding of the stories.

The stories of soaps do address our worlds and connect with our understanding; understanding their messages can for this reason tell us something about ourselves. Because of their importance in popular culture, and their variety in form around the world, soaps need to be seriously and fairly considered by analysts in terms of the stories they tell of nations and people, and the purposes they have in the lives of those who watch them.

Having sent out my clarion call in defence of the soaps, it remains only to attach one final warning. To Carol Williams's plea for analysis by people who *like* and understand the genre, I would pass on the caution Tony Warren gave me against destroying the enjoyment of the conjurer's tricks in the process of understanding them. Analysis of soaps is best when it helps viewers become literate about the form, in understanding how and why conventions of story and appearance are used, what watching and sharing them gives fans, and what soaps tell us about our lives and societies. It is also important to understand what they do not tell us: that they exaggerate some aspects of social life and downplay others for reasons of entertainment or social myth-making. But it is important that, throughout all this, we not dispel the magic. It's a fine balancing act, and as a student of mine once said, "It's a lot easier watching soaps than studying them." But understanding the form adds immeasurably to the pleasure of viewing.

Three:
The Art of the Soaps I:
The Production Machine

*N*ot *a word too many. Not a gesture needless. It is the best writing
and acting I could wish to see.*

SIR JOHN BETJEMAN,
LATE BRITISH POET LAUREATE AND PRESIDENT
OF "THE ENGLISH LEAGUE FOR HILDA OGDEN,"
ABOUT CS (NOWN 1985, BACK PAGE)

*H*ave you ever listened to the dialogue in the soaps? Truly listened? It's
bizarre!... There's no semblance of real world in it, but I still can't
leave it. I get mesmerized by them.... They're total escapism.*

COLLEEN O'TOOLE,
FAN, ABOUT AMERICAN SOAPS

SUCCESSFUL soaps can span decades on air and so can outlive their creators.
With multiple episodes shown weekly, they require a huge number of people to produce them. They must also adapt to changes in society, the television industry, and the audiences, yet must tell new stories while also
remaining faithful to their history. A long-lived soap needs fresh infusions of
producers, editors, writers, designers, even actors in order to stay alive. That
is a tall order for producers and writers, and not one shared by production
teams of prime-time series. In this chapter we look at how the wheels of the
soap machines keep turning, even when the creative torch is passed on, and
how new viewers are attracted while long-time fans are kept happy. How
do soaps change while remaining true to their roots?

Continuing serials in essence become an institution in themselves, independent of any one person. If they do not, their life span extends only so far
as their creator's interest in them. (For example, Canada's immensely popular radio serial *The Plouffe Family* ended when its creator, Roger Lemelin,

lost interest in writing it.) So a system of production was developed by soap creators fairly early, and is used relatively consistently by both American and British serials.[32] That system allows the stories to live independently of the particular individuals who brought them to life.

If a soap is going to exist in virtual perpetuity, a division of labour and a process for handing over control needs to be established, without doing damage to the vision of the original program, which, while it may shift focus, should remain intact overall. *Continuity* is the keyword. Long-term soap survival requires that the stories told at any given time be consistent with the history of the show. Therefore, the production process must obey laws internal to the story itself. For example, *GH* could not be the soap fans know if the hospital was completely removed. The creation and continuation of a soap is a world that a writer, along with producers, shapes. But what individual writers and producers can do with a soap is also determined by the show's history.

Not only does the ever-present burden of decades of story and characters impede producers and writers who want to put their personal creative stamp on their show, or simply want to improve it, it also imposes demands that are very much in tension. Too much change can destroy the consistency and history that viewers want, yet new storylines and characters must be created in order to maintain the interest of those same viewers and attract new ones. This tug-of-war is faced by both British and American producers and writers, but it takes different shapes because of the differing importance accorded to history within the two societies. Britain, with longer-standing, more entrenched testimonials to its history in its buildings and social institutions, does not value change for its own sake as much as the US does. Accordingly, British serials are, in general, more resistant to major changes in direction than are American ones. Carolyn Reynolds, former executive producer of *CS*, describes the concerns she dealt with:

> When I first started, a newspaper incorrectly quoted me as saying I was going to change a lot of things on *Coronation Street*, and I was inundated with letters and phone calls, all threatening me, saying what they'd do if I changed things. So I soon learnt that it has such a faithful following, I have to be very, very careful ... It is not what I call a producer-led programme, i.e., you don't go in and say, "I'm going to change the opening titles, I want to change the look, pace up the show or slow it down." What I can do is say I think we have too much or too little humour, I can say we have twenty scenes an episode, I'd like to take that to twenty-five to pace it up.... There are so many areas that are winners, they're working, I don't want to change for the sake of change. So you go in knowing that you have to respect this thing that has worked for thirty-odd years. (Interview)

Again, in the words of *CS*'s first executive producer, Harry Elton:

> One of the producers who took over the show early on, a man called
> Derek Granger—a man with a very distinguished career as a televi-
> sion producer—looked at me with tremendous enthusiasm when he
> was handed the assignment and said, "I can bring down the govern-
> ment!" But he couldn't. He couldn't turn it into a satire that could
> poke fun at the government. (Interview)

Elton saw, even in its early years, that the "production machine" of *CS* had
a momentum of its own, and individual writers and producers would have
to respect that (interview). Some producers, and even some analysts, see this
rigidity of form as a drawback. "There is an overdetermination of the form
that is reflected in part of [former executive producer] Susi Hush's comment in 1974 that 'it will never get to what I want to see. It's got a reality of
its own and you can't pre-empt it'" (Paterson 1981:66).

Respect for continuity of form need not, and should not, preclude
change *per se*. Change does occur as part of the natural, gradual evolution of
storytelling to match the times and the development of characters. The
more disruptive the change, however, the more likely it is, generally speaking, producer-led or ratings-led. Neither of these interventions in the natural course of a soap auger well for its narrative integrity.

Consider *CS*: its stories, characters, appearance, even the accents have
altered over the years, but those changes are more akin to the way in which
neighbourhoods evolve over decades. There are exceptions: Brian Park, who
became producer early in 1997, did shake up *CS*, "killing off" long-time
characters and introducing new young actors and steamier storylines. His
changes were not appreciated by most veteran viewers.

Still, by and large, *CS* evolves at a comparatively stately pace, with change
restrained by internal dictates. In American soaps, by contrast, historical
continuity is maintained to some extent, but drastic change of the sort
Reynolds would call "producer-led" is fairly common. Sometimes it succeeds with audiences, sometimes not.[33]

The call for change can come from even higher up, from the network
executives themselves. At these Olympian heights artistic factors play little
role, for executives typically have no creative stake in the show. Why, then,
would those at the helm risk alienating their audience by resorting to disruptive tactics? Two words that go a long way to explain this puzzle are
"impatience" and "ignorance." Networks concerned with the ratings race
may abruptly replace key personnel—making continuity of story difficult—
in order to shake up the show and, they hope, give a boost to ratings.

> During the past year, *AMC* fired its head writer, *Guiding Light* fired its head writers twice and executive producer once. *As the World Turns* fired its head writers twice and executive producer once, *Another World* fired its head writer and *two* executive producers, and *Loving* shifted its producer twice along with almost all of its writers.
>
> What is going on? Douglas Marland—the late award-winning head writer of *GL*, *General Hospital* and *ATWT*—used to say that continuity is the most important thing on daytime: "Without that, you're nothing,"Yet, many shows are ignoring that cardinal rule ...
>
> Maybe it's because slipping ratings have sparked a panic across the board, and daytime execs are understandably anxious to make changes to turn the tide. But what *kinds* of changes? (*SOD*, July 4, 1995: 28, 29)

The writer of the article quoted above sees these disruptions to a show's plotlines and characters as caused by attempts to make these shows appeal to a younger audience by increasing the number of young characters, borrowing popular storylines from other shows, regardless of whether they fit or not, and by relying too much on audience response to storylines in research focus groups and not enough on the history of the show and the storytelling vision of the writer. Rather than employing the tried-and-true, but slow method of allowing young viewers to get hooked on soaps by watching with family and friends, executives try to draw them in aggressively, to appeal to them with younger and sexier actors. The problem is that older, established characters and stories must be eliminated or backburnered in order to give air time to new youthful characters. That can alienate long-time viewers of all ages.

The dangers in this jump-starting of a slowly evolved history are well-known to viewers and perhaps to writers, but often not to network executives, who frequently come from the ranks of prime-time production. Possibly they carry the attitudes of that genre—it has to take off fast, and if it doesn't, cancel it—with them when they move to daytime. In addition, a producer or executive may want to make his or her mark as the person with the vision to create or support a television phenomenon such as *M.A.S.H.* or *Dallas*. But, in the world of soaps, while drastic change may get them some new viewers, it can cost them long-term audiences. And it is audience loyalty and longevity that has kept soaps on air for all these years, not shock-value stories. *SOD* concludes: "All this frantic firing and rehiring of the same executives is a Band-Aid at best. Effective story is what makes people watch soaps—period" (July 4, 1995: 31).

Writers and producers fired from one show are usually hired on another in a kind of soap version of musical chairs, further evidence according to *SOD* that their ability was never the issue. But perhaps that of upper-level network management is:

[Management] may be too far removed from the soap world. "They do not all like or understand soap operas," contends one long-time insider. "They tune in sporadically to see how the actors *look*. They don't understand the appeal of continuing drama.... When a network opening is created in daytime, they look outside to fill the job, rather than promoting from within. They hire someone who may not even *like* daytime. [The executives] figure: If someone is working in daytime, how good could they be?" (*SOD*, July 4, 1995: 30; emphasis in original)

This tendency to look for a quick fix, in order to compete in the all-mighty ratings race may have deeper, cultural roots. If American society, in generalized terms, is always looking for the lucky break, the winning formula, the new gimmick that will attract people and their dollars, the television industry epitomizes that tendency. Every network, every executive wants a *hit*. And in an increasingly competitive market, shows are not given time to build a viewer base. In daytime this may translate, not necessarily to cancellation of soaps as it does in prime time, but to quick fixes, whether in storylines or writer.

A second, and seemingly contradictory, tactic that arises out of the mad dash after ratings is copying someone else's success. If people like something in one version, they'll love to see it again, and again, and again. Any successful prime-time series generates clones on every network, all hoping for the same success. The temptation in the soap industry to borrow sensational stories that worked elsewhere is described by an unnamed former Procter & Gamble executive:

Last year, when *Days of Our Lives* buried [Carly] alive and the ratings temporarily jumped, [Procter & Gamble] decided that was the way to go.... Never mind that our shows have never been about that. The message we got was, "Do catfights. Have the women pull each other's hair. Have the men take their shirts off and the women loosen their blouses."...

The fact is, Carly's being buried alive by Vivian on *Days* was an innovative story that was in sync with two popular characters. It's a story that *wouldn't* work on every other show. (*SOD*, July 4, 1995: 29, 30)

Finally, relying on audience reaction to proposed storylines in focus groups means that producers may not take chances on new stories that writers want to write and that may work once they begin unfolding. Instead, direction and focus may be lost, causing disjointed stories. The result, as actress Marcy Walker (Liza on *AMC*) says, is that "the audience gets jerked around" (*SOD*, July 4, 1995, 31)

Creation of the Stories

Whether its creator remains involved or not, many more people are needed for a soap's daily development. Each soap differs from others to some extent in appearance and the types of stories told. As well, there are differences in production methods within the soap format and in production environment.[34] In general, the Americans began with the production format of radio soaps, and adapted it through trial and error to fit the medium of television, developing a method that remains largely in place to this day. The factors that influence production and story type are more diverse in the UK and occurred over a longer period of time; I will take the serials of that country as exemplar. But since *CS* and *EastEnders*, and their analyses, are reasonably well-known in North America, for the sake of freshness of presentation I will concentrate on the British serials which are less well-known on this side of the Atlantic.

One crucial difference between British and American serials, discussed at greater length in chapter five, is the significance accorded to place. England (leaving aside the nationalistic solitudes of the rest of the UK) is a collection of bounded socio-cultural entities. Towards other regions or cities Britons are suspicious and even hostile;[35] towards their own they are fiercely loyal and protective. This powerful identification with region translates into serials that are set and produced in various *identifiable* regions of the country, with their stories firmly rooted in their place of production. This has shaped the types of stories each British soap tells and led to a greater emphasis on realism of look and action. Knowing that a serial is set and made in one's own city or regions allows a more critical analysis of its relation to real life.

THE BRITISH STORIES

One of the longest-running serials, second only to *CS*, is *Emmerdale*, which is set and shot a few miles outside Leeds in a Yorkshire village. Its production offices and studios are housed in a converted wool mill. Interiors are shot there, in studio space sufficient to allow all sets to remain up at once. Exteriors are shot at locations throughout the town and at a nearby farm. The show, which started in 1972, was originally called *Emmerdale Farm* and focused on the life of a farming family. As the focus broadened, "Farm" was dropped from the name, but the farm remains important in its storylines.

Brookside, a Liverpool middle-class serial, began in 1982, the brainchild of writer Phil Redmond. Redmond wanted to write shows that accurately reflected what was going on in British society. Mal Young, one of its producers, described its beginnings:

> Phil's biggest frustration as a writer was that his work was getting taken by the large companies, and adapted.... He wasn't getting on screen ... the real passion of what he'd written. So he thought, well, the only way I'm going to do it is to own my own company.... So he set up *Brookside* in 1982, which [coincided] with the opening of Channel 4, who were looking for an anchor soap, a soap that all the rest of schedule would be aimed around, in the prime slot of eight o'clock.
>
> Phil's idea was that it would be shot very much like film, not in a studio—in real houses, with quite inexperienced actors playing closer to themselves than ever before seen on TV, almost like a documentary, really going into their lives. (Interview)

Redmond wanted *Brookside*, like his earlier writing, to be realistic in language and issues, no matter how gritty. He wanted to take the topics that mattered to individuals, communities, and the nation, the issues and concerns people talked about, and put that discourse in the mouths of the characters living in a small street. He was after something beyond *CS*, which in his opinion was a soft-edged, light look at British urban life; he wanted a harder edge approximating the lives and concerns of the people watching (Young, interview).

BBC's *EE* is set in a small working-class neighbourhood in London's east end. Discussion of social issues and the harsh realities of working-class life, have also been its leitmotif since its inception in 1985. In fact, it is criticized by viewers for being depressing and/or too topical.[36]

BBC Television did briefly turn away from high seriousness and succumb to the high life with a short-lived international entertainment. *El Dorado* was in production in the spring of 1992 with very costly and ambitious plans (Ayres, interview). Combining, in a unique way, the British taste for realism in location with the appeal of exotic glitz and glamour, the *El Dorado* team built an entire village in Spain in which its stories would be taped.[37] The soap was set in an expatriate British community on the Costa del Sol, peopled by other communities of Europeans as well as local Spaniards, a promising idea and one into which the BBC poured a lot of money. Executives banked on the notable interest Britons had shown in the sunny Australian soaps and the familiarity many have with European resort towns. They hoped that viewers would welcome *El Dorado*'s evocation of Spain's temperate climate as a palliative to the frequent tedium of British weather. But it did not work; *El Dorado* was cancelled soon after it began airing. Viewers I talked to found it "too silly."

A Granada serial also attempted to cash in on the popularity of Australian sun-and-skin afternoon soaps. *Families* is a story of two related families, one in England and one in Australia. But unlike other British soaps, both are middle and upper-middle class, and romantic entanglements are central to the structure. Its late afternoon and late night (repeat) time slots mean smaller audiences than the prime-time giants. According to Carolyn Reynolds, a former producer of it as well as of *CS*, its airtime and romantic focus attract a higher proportion of women viewers, along with retirees and shift workers (interview).[38]

Because British serials are localized, a true-to-life fictionalizing of an identifiable area, with the story reflecting to some extent the way of life and specific interests of the region in which they are made, one region is unlikely to successfully market more than one soap. Concern for authenticity of "voice" means that a Tony Warren or Phil Redmond would be unlikely to create a soap set outside the region they know. So there are no soap empire-builders in the UK. One "institution" seems enough to satisfy British writers who, like Tony Warren, may continue to write, but in a different genre (in his case, novels).

AMERICAN SOAP WRITERS

In contrast to British localized soaps and soaps creators and perhaps reflective of the ethos of build and build big, many American soap writers made careers, and empires, out of the soaps. Creators of American soaps concentrate less on geographical place and more on the emotional lives of their characters. They have been less concerned with reflecting the social realities of the middle America about which they write than with the inner life of relationships and family. And so, in these soaps produced in New York or Los Angeles, multinational corporations and crime syndicates have their operations in small middle-American cities; social circles of millionaire CEOs include every occupational and social class; and ordinary people are regularly kidnapped, threatened with death, and charged with murder. They commit acts of violence, suffer amnesia, and rapidly become raving drug addicts. Usually several such dramatic occurrences happen at the same time. As Robert Rorke writes:

> Characters come back from the dead all the time. They recover from "fatal" diseases, endure more than one bout of amnesia, give birth when they're well past middle age and constantly "meet" children they never knew they had. But ... you won't ... find dentists listed in a soap town's Yellow Pages. (*SOD*, December 8, 1992: 75)

Far more farfetched plots than amnesia or long-lost children or siblings have played out on American soaps: an alien visitor to Port Charles; characters falling through a tunnel back in time to the American frontier on *OLTL* (three years after the 1985 movie *Back to the Future*), then a year later creating an underground "lost city" called Eterna. Perhaps most outlandish of all is the 1995 *DOOL* story in which Marlena was possessed by the devil and could transform herself into other people or monstrous shapes. One reason why American viewers accept even the most fantastic plots, although they may not like them, is that non-specificity of place makes approximation to reality less important. We do not live in Port Charles, we do not know what might happen in that world, but we may enjoy science-fiction and horror movies. The way soaps intersperse fantastic stories with "everyday life" gives us both.

The lessened emphasis on geography may also underlie the inclination of American writers to create more than one soap. Many internal worlds can be envisaged and brought to life when they are not dominated by physical space, not tied to one particular plot of land and its limited environs. Also, perhaps, centralized production locations and facilities aid individuals in developing multiple soaps. And the prime-time production company tendency to empire-build may spill over to daytime when both industries work in the same area.

Current American soaps are the visions of a handful of people. Irna Phillips, the grand doyenne of soap opera, created radio and then television soaps, among them the still-running *AW*, *ATWT*, *DOOL*, and *GL*. Her protegée, Agnes Nixon, created *AMC* and *OLTL*. Both created many more long- and short-running soaps that no longer air. *GH* is the product of Frank and Doris Hursley. Finally, Bill and Lee Phillip Bell created *Y&R* and *B&B*. Prime-time television producer Aaron Spelling entered the daytime world with *Sunset Beach*.

Because her output was so prodigious, the late Irna Phillips epitomizes the writer who creates a story, sees it on its way to survival, and turns to the creation of another, slightly different, story. But Phillips never fully gave up control. Cantor and Pingree describe her system of working: "According to some reports, she wrote over 2 million words a year. Using a large month-by-month word chart, Phillips plotted and wrote as many as six soaps at once, dictating the action to her secretary" (1983: 43).

Bill Bell is a present-day soap creator who also maintains continued hands-on control. The Bells' production company, along with Columbia Pictures, owns *Y&R* and their newer soap, *B&B*. *Y&R* in particular has done its creators credit: it has consistently ranked first in many American and Canadian markets, and it, as well as *B&B*, are top-rated programs in Italy, Greece, and elsewhere in Europe.

Bell's soaps are a family business. He was executive producer of both and was head writer of *Y&R* since its inception in 1972 until early 1998 when he turned to development of a new soap. His wife, Lee Phillip Bell, is a production partner; son Bradley is executive producer and head writer of *B&B*; and daughter Lauralee plays Christine Williams on *Y&R*. Melody Thomas Scott, *Y&R*'s Nikki, is the wife of *Y&R* director Edward Scott. Laura Bryan Birn, Paul William's faithful, love-lorn secretary Lynn on *Y&R*, is the daughter of *Y&R* writer Jerry Birn.

Bell extends the longevity of characters and storylines by cross-fertilization of shows. He can interweave the people of Genoa City (*Y&R*) with the Forrester family of *B&B*—characterization and production can be fused more easily—because he owns both shows. Switching of actors and stories between related soaps is not new—*AW* had cross-overs to spin-off shows *Somerset* and *Texas*; *AMC*'s Jeremy went from that show to the defunct *Loving*; *GH* characters moved to its 1997 spin-off *Port Charles*. Cross-over of plots and performers allows continuity of history and character while adding new twists. And it can increase audience numbers, as it did strikingly for *B&B*: many fans of *Y&R*'s conniving lunatic, Sheila, added *B&B* to their viewing roster when she began causing mayhem on that show.

Creating CS

In Britain, the most successful serial and the bench-mark for soap creation is Tony Warren's *CS*, produced and set in Salford, twin city of Manchester. Warren still lives in Manchester and writes novels based on the life of that city. He watches *CS*; indeed, he grins, he is "the only person who is paid to watch [it]" (interview). He is a consultant to Granada, and his part in the program is acknowledged in the credits: "based on an original idea by Tony Warren." Warren wrote the first thirteen-week series never expecting that he was setting in motion a social phenomenon. Nor did he want it to take over his life, "I laid the foundation stones, but, make no mistake, today it's a team effort.... But I'm a solo performer ... just a different kind of writer" (interview). Even after he stopped writing it, however, it engulfed him:

> [I] couldn't turn to the court pages [of the newspaper] without reading "She came from a *Coronation Street*-type background. I remember a morning sitting on a bus [overhearing] two women [saying] ... "Did you see it last night?" I thought, I'll never escape this thing! (Interview)

Strangely, the publicity and the literature on *CS* rarely mention the pivotal role Harry Elton played in creating the "British institution," as it is often called. Yet, with Warren, Elton worked against considerable odds within and outside Granada in order to get "a home-grown serial" on air. The story of *CS*, told in the words of these two men, is quite as engaging as any of its episodes.[39]

> Elton: Granada was trying to develop local programming in accordance with government regulations about local content on the new private, commercial networks. I remembered the soap operas I had seen when growing up in Canada and later in Detroit. I knew that they were extremely popular, and that production costs were lower because the same sets could be used over and over and actors could be signed on long contracts.
>
>   There was this kid writing for Granada, *Captain Biggles* and other series. He had a way of hearing Manchester/Salford talk. I asked him to write a pilot and outline for a thirteen-week season about life in the north. He went away, and came back with the first episode of *Coronation Street*.
>
> Warren: I invented it out of sheer desperation.... I was adapting novels of Captain W.E. Johns [Biggles], which I found fascist and incomprehensible. I said [to Elton], let me write what I know about, show business. He said that's the kiss of death [for television] ... [I said] I know about the north of England, and more to humour me than anything else he said go away and come back in twenty-four hours with a show that'll take the world by the ears ...

So the pilot episode of a serial was written and shot. Its name was long debated. Warren favoured a name of the romantic type common in the Victorian vintage row-house streets he was writing about. "Florizel Street" was his choice, but it was discarded when "the tea lady said it sounded like a disinfectant." After discussion of another popular type of name commemorating Queen Victoria's sixty-year reign, "Coronation Street" won out over "Jubilee Street." While Elton and Warren were delighted with their product, studio executives, when they saw it, were not so sure of its value or saleability.

> Elton: I remember after the pilot was shown ... they sat down to pronounce. The first man, who was an American variety person, said: That's a soap opera! You don't put that crap on

at seven o'clock at night, you put that on in the daytime.

Cecil Bernstein ... said: Harry, you've made a horrible mistake, and we can't blame you because you're a Canadian.... North Country accents are the language of George Formby and Old Mother Riley. And whenever people hear it, they laugh. They'll never take it seriously.

The general manager, who had been working with Korda in film, said: There's not a single thing I like about that program; I don't like the characters, I don't like the sets, and I don't like the stories. Surely people watch television to be taken out of their dreary lives, not to have their noses rubbed into reality!

Warren: Harry Elton refused to be defeated.... He set up monitors all round the studio. And he sent out memos to everybody from the chairman down to the cleaners and said, today at one o'clock, we will be showing two episodes of a home-grown serial that we believe in. We would like you to watch it and fill in questionnaires.

The reactions to these questionnaires were exactly the same as the reactions have always been ever since to *Coronation Street*: the people either loved it or they loathed it, but they didn't feel indifferently about it. The ones who loved it far outweighed the ones who loathed it. And so it was the people who got the show onto the air, not the powers that be! The people and a Canadian!

Elton: Just as all my distinguished colleagues felt that the show wouldn't work, the critics, all of them I think,... knocked that show....⁴⁰ Television was important enough, and there were only the two channels, so that everybody wrote on it—it was in *The Times, The Observer, The Guardian*.

There was a young Canadian who was writing television criticism for one of the distinguished weeklies.... He said: This is pap! This is what Lenin was talking about when he talked about religion—it was the opium of the people—Granada are now putting out this crap to make the working classes, who are the victims of British society, feel contented in their miserable lot. That Canadian's name was Mordecai Richler.

While critics opined, Elton dealt with studio brass, and Warren expanded his characters and street. In the first episode, he introduced a character who would become the second-best-known woman in the UK: Ena Sharples.

The casting of the late Violet Carson in that role is a wonderfully serendipitous story:

> Warren: The original Ena was, to a certain extent, my maternal grandmother. [She] was a very commanding woman. She commanded because she'd been a great beauty in her day ... she refused to concede it was for a moment over and she thought she should get her own way by divine right.
>
> Violet was not a beauty by any stretch of the imagination, but trying to get her own way, because she was really such an unprepossessing-looking person, worked in an odd way just the same ...
>
> [A] week before we were due to go on the air I was told, well, you've written this part, but it's uncastable; you've written a woman in her seventies with the energy of a girl of nineteen and you're going to have to cut it. But I said, I really can't cut it ... she's a linchpin ... I said, well there's always Vi. I'd known her in *Children's Hour* on the radio where I began as a boy actor.... She was a tough old biddy and I wasn't sure I wanted any more of it, to be quite honest.... And they debated whether it was worth bringing her from Blackpool and paying her third-class rail fare ... to be camera-tested.
>
> But anyway, she came over and did one run-through on camera and she wasn't very good. And then she did a second one and I kissed the screen!... [The director] said, in the first one she did what I was telling her to do, in the second one she just went her own sweet way! And that was Violet.... For many people she *was Coronation Street*.

The calibre of its acting and writing, and the realism of its depiction of northern life—in characterization, dialogue, and situation—made *CS* unique and enormously successful in British programming.

> Elton: [Tony's] ability [was] to reflect the way people really talked, but with a sharp edge ... [E]verywhere he went on buses he would have a pencil and a piece of paper and he would listen to people talk, and write down what they said.... So he set the style...; it was real people talking to each other about real problems.... [W]hen you have that kind of reality, it has a universality about it that lets it jump over borders.

And jump borders it has: *CS* is exported worldwide. It has long been popular in New Zealand, Australia, Canada, and many other countries. British expatriates watch it for a glimpse of home, but many with no associations with the UK are faithful viewers. Its stories of people translate across accent, lifestyle, and culture.

The history of *CS* illustrates how a soap was created; it now needed to lay the foundation for its continuation. The machine of team writing and production, respecting the character of its past while permitting change, is the key to that longevity. A similar system is used by American soaps, To see how the machine works there, let us look at *AW.*

Staying Alive: AW

The pressure to deliver well-written, interesting stories is great for all soap writers. But in the US the demands placed on them (as well as on actors to deliver quality performances) are double those on British writers, for all American soaps air five days a week, and most are one hour in length. In the UK, by contrast, serials are half-an-hour in length and air only two or three times weekly, with *CS* going to four days a week only late in 1996. Creating a serial and developing stories that appeal to enough viewers to build a viable audience base is difficult enough; continuing to tell interesting and new stories, within the confines of a particular show's history and character base even from one season to the next, tests the creative mettle of any writer. This challenge is far weightier for the daytime soaps. Prime-time soap producers can keep a hit serial like *Beverly Hills 90210* on air for as long as ratings hold, or until they decide to let it die an honourable death. They can then go on to create another fictional world that suits their taste, or their perception of audience tastes. Daytime serials, and their audiences, are a bit different and cannot be treated so blithely. Getting a new soap off the ground means taking viewers away from their usual daily routine; and stories with a thirty- or forty-year history have a different kind of viewer loyalty than prime time, where seven or eight seasons counts as a very long run.

Soap writers, as we have seen, must work within the confines of their show's history. Some characters and families may have been on air for decades, indeed some since the very first broadcast. The long-term characters must be integrated with newcomers and must continue to have their own interesting, but not too repetitive, stories. It is a hard thing to do, and therefore stories are recycled. With limited time available for coming up with ideas and framing them in innovative language, soap dialogue can suffer. Critics of soaps call the writing "formulaic," and it often is. Such critics tend to assume this is because the soaps hire hack writers. But stilted and repetitive dialogue may equally well be the result of the time constraints under which writers and production teams labour. Writers must produce vast amounts of dialogue for each episode,[41] and American writers churn out five episodes a week. As well as the daunting pace of writing, writers must come up with realistic but interesting plots in stories that have continued for decades. Formulaic writing might well be caused by the weight of so many years of storyline dogging the heels of every new idea. Soap writers are constantly trying to find a viable balance between the need for continuity and the need for change, as well as new stories and new ways to retell stories, so it shouldn't surprise us if the attempt to appease both results in some sacrifice of quality.

To compound their problems, soap writers are not just writing one major plotline. At any given time, there are two or three major storylines and another two or three minor plots. Story development must be juggled with ratings concerns and with actors' contracts and events in their personal lives. Soap writers must cope with all these, sometimes conflicting, pressures while creating stories that appeal to new viewers and maintain consistency with the past so as not to alienate long-standing fans. How do they do it? Donna Swajeski, former head writer at *AW*, describes the process:

> Basically, on our show there's one head writer, and it's usually my vision that guides the show in terms of creative ideas. I have a staff of eight writers. Four of them are what are called "outline writers" or "plottists." They sit with me, and when I lay out each day they write an outline of it. Because we have a very, very standard form of six acts, certain teasers, tags that everything has to be put into, to make sure it makes an hour's show. Then it's handed to script writers, who basically sit at home and they each are assigned a day and they write from those outlines. Then I edit everything to make sure that everything was exactly ... how I saw it in the beginning ...
>
> I have final approval with the writers and then, when I've finished a week, I sit down with NBC and with Procter & Gamble and the producer, and we hash it out together. We all pretty much have an equal say. But ultimately it's between the producer and the writer: what he can put on the screen and what I can write. (Interview)

Writers try not to let actors' personalities unduly influence the nature of the characters they portray. They focus on those characters as they envisioned them:

> I keep away from the actors as much as I can because I create a story persona for these people. It's better not to really know them. For

example, there's a lot of little things sometimes that creep in: like you'll be writing a super-couple and maybe [the actors who play them] are not really getting along. We want to keep away from a lot of that. (Swajesky, interview)

Viewer response also affects writers' stories to some extent. If fans stop watching because of unpopular pairings or stories, the soap is in trouble. Producers monitor fan mail and pay attention to Neilsen data, magazine surveys, and cyberspace discussion groups. Some also use focus group research, in which an independent facilitator asks a small group of fans for reactions to existing, and potential, storylines.

Depending on who you talk to, focus groups are either one of the most valuable research tools at a network's disposal or one of the worst things that ever happened to daytime ... *TV Guide* soap colum-nist Michael Logan [says] "The true artists, like ... Bill Bell don't want anything to do with focus groups. And that makes sense. A painter would not let you stand behind him and tell him where to put the dab of blue ...

[Executive producer Jill Farren] Phelps believes that focus group opinions are most valuable when a show's writers are at a crossroads. "... the focus groups can help you understand the audience's wishes."... Fine-tuning a storyline is fine and dandy, but Phelps, play-ing devil's advocate, cautions against letting the participants' opinions interfere too drastically with the writers' vision. "You don't want writing by committee," she sighs. "It's dangerous when a writer does-n't go with his own instincts." (*SOD*, October 10, 1995: 54–57)

Yet perusal of any of the e-mail soap newsgroups will show that what fans want as much or more than interesting stories is consistency of story history and character. Most are willing to sit out plots that bore or annoy them, but many draw the line at too many rapid changes in storyline focus and at "uncharacteristic" behaviour. For instance, on the newsgroup that discusses *AW*, Jill Farren Phelps came in for vociferous criticism for the changes she made in the show, which backburnered, eliminated, or significantly altered long-established characters.

One reason why consistency of character is an issue for fans is that soap characters are as well-known to them as friends and family. Just as with real people, then, their attitudes and actions can often be predicted. So when they do something not in keeping with their "personality" the audience, at the very least, notices. Characters can and of course do change. *AW*'s evil Carl Hutchins, for instance, reformed, but the reasons for this were made clear, and he kept enough of his dark side to have his character continue to be interesting and believable.[42] In contrast, many viewers were annoyed when former executive producer Phelps's sidelined the central family, the Corys, by new characters she introduced.

Another reason that fans insist on a certain consistency of characterization is that, just as we all do of the people we meet in real life, soap fans like some characters more than others. A particular storyline may bore one person because of its events or characters, but that person will continue to watch the serial if there are enough other stories and characters to engage him or her.[43] Too many radical deviations from what the viewer has tuned in to see—too many ruptures in characterization or storyline—and the viewer will cease to recognize in the serial the sources of pleasure he or she seeks.[44]

Backstage

Soaps require much more than writers and actors to appear on air. The ambience of a soap is created by technical crews responsible for set design, costume, and make-up in addition to camera work and lighting. Every soap has a small army of technical people whose efforts make the characters and stories work, and not just in the obvious ways. Music can suit the atmosphere of a scene; set design can avoid awkward navigation around furniture or lamps. Technical effects also act as a visual form of story continuity. Every family and individual has their distinctive setting and look, and on American daytime shows, couples and types of scenes often have their own theme music. With sets known to us already, even if a scene opens with an empty room, we know who will come in and where the action is taking place. On a larger scale, each soap has its own "look" that subtly differentiates it and provides continuity over time. These are all the products of an efficient team of technical people.

The work of technicians succeeds if it is not noticed, if it does not divert attention from the actors and dialogue. The technical demands are fierce, for the nature of the genre means more rapid *everything* than in prime-time television or film. Endless fiddling and retakes are not possible. With actors and dialogue forming the basis of the dramatic action, and the likeliest source of fumbling, no one wants to waste time redoing sets, makeup, or costume. In the early days, as we saw in chapter one, sets were minimal, even flimsy; there are industry jokes about walls shaking or even falling down when doors were closed. As late as the latter 1970s, sets were, in Carol Williams' opinion, overdressed and "downright tacky," and shot with very poor lighting (1992: 32). Thankfully, increased budgets for sets and new camera and lighting equipment has permitted more sophistication in daytime's look.

Discussion of all aspects of technical production is beyond the scope of this study.[45] I will confine my comments to technical construction of the overall look of a show and of individual characters. As always in both American and British serials, characters take the lead: according to Williams, sets remain the same for long periods of time not only out of budgetary constraints and because viewers like familiarity of surroundings, but because the emphasis in soaps is on the characters, not the scenery. Details of both clothing and housing are selected to reveal aspects of a character's "personality," as well as his or her social circumstance and position.

Clothing changes more rapidly than building interiors because soaps want to stay on top of fashions in dress and hair styles: viewers rely on them for fashion guidance and interesting new "looks" they might like to try. "[Fans] learn from [the soaps], they say: what styles and colors are new and would look good on 'me.' This goes for the men, too—Jeremy's [of *AMC*] sweaters elicited as many enquiries as Natalie's or Erica's outfits" (Williams 1992: 78).

Clothes are bought off the rack and are mixed and matched for new looks with the same pieces, just as we do ourselves with our own wardrobes. Soap characters, however, are more likely than most of us to have designer gowns specially-made for their formal occasions, and the price-tags can be hefty (Delgado interview)

The actor's tastes and personality could influence his or her character's appearance. Linda Dano (Felicia on *AW*) designs clothes in addition to her acting career and she has often "dressed" Felicia in her own designs (Dano, interview).

Alice Barrett (formerly Frankie Frame, *AW*) describes in an *SOD* interview how she influenced her character's development. Frankie Frame was a New Age-type character possessing ESP and interested in all things mystical. Barrett wore her own crystal earring and necklace to her screen test, and they were incorporated into Frankie's "look." She told the story of how another aspect of Frankie's persona came to be. A scene called for her to eat a hot dog. In real life a vegetarian who refuses to eat red meat, no matter how processed the product, Barrett asked for anything else. "And then someone decided that it would be funnier if Frankie went down and ordered a bun full of sauerkraut. And so that's when the vegetarianism got dropped in" (*SOD*, December 8, 1992: 20).

Like clothing styles, sets are designed to illustrate the nature of the characters utilizing them. Places of employment are generally restricted to signalling a character's vocation and the business's type and level of prosperity, but homes can be used to provide a visual representation of the personalities of the characters who live there—darkly elegant with lots of leather and mahogany for rich men with expensive tastes; large, light kitchens and comfortable living rooms for down-to-earth family people—living spaces are used to reinforce the persona projected by the actor.

Set designer Bobby Burke thinks through a character in order to come up with the right ambience for his or her house (interview). Burke designed the home of *AW*'s Carl Hutchins, an urbane Englishman with a criminal past and the soul of a poet. Conniving, ruthless, and independently wealthy, Hutchins was an engaging antihero who accepted only the best of artistic and material comforts. Before Carl mended his ways (partially), married Rachel Cory, and moved to the Cory mansion, Burke reflected the character's love of Shakespeare, opera, and Oriental art in the creation of an elegant sculpture- and book-filled residence. It, and the persona of a soft-spoken and soft-footed Asian manservant Ito, deftly complemented Carl's character. After moving to the Cory mansion, Carl made it his own in subtle ways. For instance, in the June 4, 1996 episode, operatic music played while he and Rachel talked. But it was not overlaid, perfect-quality sound, mixed in during production as is customary on soaps. It was more distant, sounding as if the couple had turned on the stereo in the room. It reminded us of a defining aspect of Carl we had not seen much of since he married Rachel, and it helped make her space his. This example also shows how continuity can coexist with the new. In Rachel's story, much has changed over the past decade. The death of Douglass Watson, her on-screen husband Mac Cory, meant new story directions had to be written for her. But her physical domestic space did not change: characters, as well as actors and viewers, are reminded of Mac and Watson by his photo prominently displayed in the living room. The reuniting of Rachel and Carl in a new way—domestic harmony—evoked the stormy history of enmity between Carl and the Corys. Adding touches of Carl's personality to Rachel's home, with its reminders of Mac, integrated their new story into the setting of long-established characters and story history.

One hallmark of American soaps that greatly influences their design and production is that they are shot almost entirely inside studios—location shoots are relatively infrequent. Hence the sets and camera methods must create the illusion of spaciousness in tiny spaces. The sets Burke designs are small, maybe eight-by-ten-foot cubicles lined side-by-side in a large sound stage. The day I visited the *AW* studio, the Cory mansion gazebo set was up—part of it, only one side attached to the wall, with artificial trees alongside, which is all we ever see on screen. Next was the Cory dining room, with barely enough space to squeeze behind the chairs. Amanda Cory's bedroom was crowded with a large four-poster bed and dressers all cheek-by-jowl. But when translated to our screens, these tiny rooms look like the spacious quarters one would expect in a mansion.

On the other side of the Cory quarters was a short-term set on which three rows of three or four cinema seats were lined up—nothing else. The scene being shot involved Michael Hudson taking Rachel Cory to a movie. Being a millionaire, he of course rented the entire theatre, so only enough seats to convey emptiness around them were needed. I watched with special interest when that scene aired, and yes, on screen it did look like a large and empty theatre!

British Serials

As noted above, the basic methods of writing and production are similar in British and American serials, but there are differences rooted in the British use of more non-studio shots. Scheduling is one such difference. *CS* shoots its street scenes and location shots at the beginning of the week so that interiors shot later will match: "so if it is raining on Monday, when they're in studio three days later, we put raindrops on their shoulders" (Mares, interview). *Emmerdale* has four-legged actors as well as two-legged to consider, which causes unique production problems. The farm they use for exteriors was initially a working dairy farm, and so the cows became accustomed to the actors and camera crews, making taping of milking scenes and so on relatively painless. But the farmer/owner retired and sold his herd. Cows then had to be trucked in when needed. Not being actor cows, they caused considerable difficulties by stampeding off in the wrong direction when the actors and camera crew approached them (Turner, interview). Such are the perils of realism! Because *Brookside* uses the interiors of real houses, their camera techniques deviate from the standard method of the invisible "fourth wall" that a three-sided studio set uses:

> We're based right in the middle of a ... housing estate that's been in existence for ten years. All over Britain have been popping up all these brand-new housing estates with a good mix of different styles of houses.... So we wanted to reflect that, so we bought six of the houses in the middle of this housing estate. We didn't really adapt them, other than the fact that you can plug your camera and your sound cables into a little box underneath the stairs. Other than that, they're normal houses.... And all these cables ... go underground to one of the houses inside [which] we've got a standard recording gallery, equipment, makeup, wardrobe, production office. (Young, interview)

The fact that British serials, with the exception of *EE,* are made in the same place as they are set makes them more accessible to their viewers. It is possible to visit them and see where and how they are made. This, combined with a more realistic look due in part to the use of real spaces, make some people wonder if they could do better. Probably all soap fans have thought about the soap that *they* would write, but New York and Los Angeles are other worlds for those of us living in the North American hinterland. Nothing akin to this constrains viewers in the UK. At one Liverpool pub, the landlord thought that the lives of his patrons were at least as interesting as the fictional lives on British serials. He set out to do something about it.

LIFEBOYS

The Shipperies is a pub in Wavertree, a suburb of Liverpool, operated by Pat O'Rourke and his wife Agnes. Like many British pubs, it is over 300 years old, according to its owner:

> Its character is within the walls. Downstairs [in the pub] we only ever paint, we will never alter the structure because there's so much there of the past.... Everybody knows that this is their pub, it's the way their grandfathers remember it, and their children coming up ... When I'm talking to them, they'll tell me about when such and such a body sat in that far corner, and they're talking about their grandparents. (O'Rourke, interview)

If the pub itself is a neighbourhood institution, so too are many of its patrons. "Lifeboys" is the nickname given to the young and not-so-young men who visit it after work.

The pub is divided into two parts. The smaller "parlour" is frequented on a Friday night by older patrons (known as the "wrinklies"), bingo games are held there, and patrons generally gather there to sit and talk. The larger room is louder and rowdier. It is where bands play on the nights entertainment is offered and where the "lifeboys" usually gather.

Like most Britons, the O'Rourkes and their customers watch the serials. And like all "scousers" (Liverpudlians), they are very proud of their city, especially its people's humour, creative use of language, and friendliness. What they saw on *Brookside*, also set in Liverpool, did not impress them; they considered it a negative portrayal of the city as too violent and inaccurate in depicting the "ordinary" concerns of Britons and British society.

They felt the same way about *CS*. Pat O'Rourke indicating the size of his pub, said that it, several times the size of the Rovers Return and with a steady clientele, did not provide enough money to afford "jetting off to Europe on vacation the way [the Rovers' owners] do." He gently chastened me for my credulity in believing the *CS* storylines: "And they tell you it was real life, and you believe them! Mind you, in America they got Disneyland

and everybody believes that's true as well!"[46]

So, in 1992, O'Rourke, who has a background in camera work and operates an actor-casting agency, decided to make his own soap, based on the real lives of his patrons. He, with co-writer and actor Paul McCann, talked about the evolution of *Lifeboys* from pub entertainment (essentially home video: taping people in the pub and playing it back for them) to a scripted, casted soap looking for a national venue.

> *O'Rourke*: We had entertainment on all the time ... so I was thinking of a new method for bringing more people in.... So first one we did was on a camcorder.... When we put it on, somebody contacted somebody in the media.... Next minute we was inundated with calls about our soap. We used to look forward to seeing it every Wednesday night.... We'd write the scripts down but not in the detail as we're doing now. It was just for fun, and then everybody would be in and watching themselves on the TV..."

Originally, pub patrons portrayed themselves. But O'Rourke found that some people were camera shy and others could not be themselves on camera effectively.

> *O'Rourke*: They sound great when they're talking, because they're talking directly to you. But as soon as you put a camera lens on them, something seems to happen. I don't know what it is, they seem to go cold, tend to stutter more.... When they see themselves on a monitor, you can see the colour just drain from their face. Then they start altering their face slightly to get the best profile....
>
> That was taking it away from what we wanted to do, we wanted to do a soap that looked real, that we could do better than anybody else and entertain ourselves a bit with it.... We found that they had bigger stories to tell, not just for the fun now. They wanted us to tell a story, their story, but not people just to be running around having a laugh and joke.... So we started talking to them every day and putting it on tape. And then doing the script and letting them read it, and "yeah, that's exactly what it was like, but *I* said that, she didn't."... Some things we've got in the script they don't know where we got it from. And normally, it's from their sons or daughters.... So they're seeing little shock bits on the screen that they didn't know was gonna go in. So again, it's a kind of candid camera within a soap.

With his casting agency list, O'Rourke assembled actors to portray many of the pub patrons, but a few still played themselves:

O'Rourke: Jimmy's about eighty now, and to him and his grandkids he's a star, and why not?... Every time he's in it, his whole family is in, all watching their grandpa saying "hello there Tom," ... something like that, and it's made his day.

After collecting the histories of their patrons/characters, the writers developed their stories. They were constantly supplied with new material because the people they were writing about continued to have new events unfold in their lives.

McCann: We have to sit with the customers as regular as possible, so we can keep generating further storylines.... Most of the ideas come from Pat's head because ... he knows all these people inside out. But I've slowly got to know them just as well myself, so I can chip in now and then with an idea.... He walks around and the characters take over him, and that's how we do it.

With camera equipment provided by a local businessman, they could, when necessary, shoot an episode a day.

McCann: A typical day will start about nine in the morning ... talking over storylines and how we should use them within the context of future stories we're building up to. Eventually the idea comes about, and that's it. We're just frantic for about eight hours writing a script, and it's virtually complete ... [On a] typical day, we're here till half past two in the morning ...
     Then we plot and plan our locations and for the future and set them up ... We go through a full day's rehearsal on every script ... and this morning, the scene itself, to actually shoot and get in the can, was half an hour ... We can really compete with anybody else, TV-wise, acting-wise, film-wise, everything.

There was extensive media coverage of *Lifeboys*, and O'Rourke and the cast hoped for a network offer to put it on air.[47] The show caught the attention of national and international media because it was an obvious, but wonderfully fresh, idea. In watching soaps, we are watching the daily life of fictional people who become as well-known to us as our friends. Pat O'Rourke simply extended that to present the lives of real people. The ultimate objective was to present their stories to the entire nation.

> *McCann*: I think we're different from *Brookside* because our storylines are taken from real people.... We've met the people, we know them personally, we're writing about them and what's happened to them. The writers of *Brookside*—and any other soaps for that matter—the writers couldn't possibly have met all these characters that are in their soaps.

> *O'Rourke*: Producers of TV programs ... try to create a fictional world where they can take the people out of the humdrum of their life and put them into a fantasy side of life ... [but it's making] fun of people by creating something around them that doesn't exist, because they can't relate to it. They can't say, "That was me." How many soaps have you seen where somebody's knocked on the door and said, "Can you lend me the price of a loaf until me husband comes in?"... [But] where have you ever seen it where people are borrowing money just for ale? The betting shop? You never see that ... but that is real life! So in a way I think we've caused a revolution in the way TV production should be done.... It's a new approach and everybody applauds us on what we do.

Well, not everyone. Some real-life lifeboys were less enthusiastic.

The "lads," the lifeboys, had freely wandered between the small parlour and the larger public room. But during the taping of *Lifeboys* the parlour was used as the main set. Although Pat said all were free to wander in at any time, some of the real lifeboys felt the room had become off-limits to them. One said, "The family's made it, just made it up. Because we've all been pushed out of the parlour, pushed into the bar. But *we're* the bar crew that's in here all the time, like." Some also felt that O'Rourke was telling the stories *he* wanted to tell, and those stories did not accurately reflect the real people's lives. What "reality" in entertainment television means to viewers is complex and multi-layered, even when the producers and production centres are in cities known as entertainment capitals and when their fictional cities are transparently fictional. When the production occurs in your own backyard, or local pub, and writers, actors, and "characters" all know each other, understanding the interplay of fictional entertaining with accurate representation of social life becomes even more difficult.

Lifeboys was, ironically, ordinary people's attempt to make realistic, localized soaps even more real. Actor John Costane explained:

A lot of [soaps] are based in fictional towns, so people can't say, well, people from Longchester wouldn't say that, because there's no such place anyway, so you can get away with it.... We're not knocking the programs or the quality of the acting, just the realism of it. (Interview)

Costane's criticism was directed to *CS*, where not all actors are from Manchester/Salford even though their characters were supposedly born there. But *CS*'s Salford is called Weatherfield, a fictional town very close to Manchester, a proximity made clear by, for example, characters who go to Manchester for dinner. Still, as Costane pointed out, because Weatherfield doesn't exist, its residents needn't muster the authenticity of dialect that the *Lifeboys* team found so crucial: those involved with *Lifeboys* insisted that Liverpudlian characters speak with authentic scouser accents. Clearly, that team would be dismayed by the often very odd pastiche of dialects to be found within the cities of American soaps.[48]

Pat O'Rourke started with real people and their real lives on camera. That changed to actors presenting the real lives of people likely to be watching the product. It further evolved into hopes for those actors to portray real people's lives for the nation. While based on real people's lives, the stories are summarized and edited for effective storytelling; after all, just presenting the routine of day-to-day life would be very boring. Despite wanting to present "reality," then, Pat O'Rourke concentrated on the interesting bits of people's lives in order to tell good stories. His stories may include more gritty bits of daily British working-class existence than do the others, but can one say they are real?

When I first heard the story of *Lifeboys* (in an interview with Pat O'Rourke, *As It Happens*, CBC Radio, December 10, 1991), I was delighted: people making their own television, telling their own stories! But if actors are *portraying* those real people, and O'Rourke and McCann are writing scripts *based on* the lives of those people, is it those people telling their stories, or is it more akin to Warren putting his grandmother's words or overheard conversations into the mouths of fictional characters?

Here is another way of making the same point. When I spoke with him, O'Rourke said that they had devised the following way of avoiding any apparent religious affiliation on the show: the vicar's character was a composite of the neighbourhood Roman Catholic and Church of England priests, a blending of two different theologies and personalities into one. *That is what fiction writers do.*

I asked Pat O'Rourke if he was fictionalizing his own pub and clientele. He said no: "If I was going to fictionalize it, I would give it another name, and then hopefully try to draw a character into that. But the Shipperies is exactly what it is." But it is the reality of the Shipperies and the lifeboys as Pat O'Rourke and Paul McCann decided to present it. It is a considered delivery of a social reality, which *may* only more closely approximate real life in Liverpool than its competitor *Brookside*. This is not to say O'Rourke's experiment with "real-life" soaps is not valuable; it is. But the nature of enjoying television, and perhaps all storytelling, is that we want the boring bits left out. Television stories, even "factual" documentaries, require a degree of dramatization and encapsulation in order to tell their stories and not be just unedited tape footage.

Conclusion

Soap operas cannot simply be one person's artistic vision, not if they are going to survive indefinitely. Even a writer who never becomes bored with his or her creation needs a writing and production staff to supplement the driving vision and stand ready to take over when the show's creator has had enough. Certainly, if the machine had not been in place in 1961, when Warren stopped writing *CS*, that serial would not be on the air today.

Soap writers have to work at a dizzying pace. Even in the UK, where soaps air at most four times weekly,[49] in total air-time that is close to a full-length movie a *week*. American writers must produce five hours of story every week. In addition, all writers have to continue to develop new and interesting stories for long-term characters as they bring in new ones.

Fans, especially of American soaps, are quite forgiving of repetitious or hackneyed storylines. This is not to suggest that they accept bad writing or continuity lapses quietly, only that it takes a lot for them to give up on their favourite stories. And they know the pressures under which writers and technicians are working. British fans expect greater realism in story and appearance in their serials, and that is what they get.

British serials follow, for the most part, the same writing and production method used by American soaps. An important difference is time; having half-hour episodes two or three times weekly allows more time for writing, rehearsals, and taping. But British serials use more local outside shots than American ones, making for differences in production scheduling.

Soap writers and producers who succeed respect the history of their story and their characters, and they respect the fans. *AW* and Proctor & Gamble perhaps are paying the price for alienating fans by making too many changes, with too many departures of long-time, favourite actors/characters. Fans have stopped watching the show and even stopped buying Proctor & Gamble's products. E-mail newsgroups speculate that NBC wants an excuse to cancel the show in order to make scheduling room for a new network-owned soap created by former *DOOL* head writer James Reilly; annoying fans to the point that they give up on their show would make this cancellation easier. The fans suspect a cynical manipulation of them, and many have given up caring. The "friendship" they had with the denizens of *AW*'s Bay City no longer outweighs their feeling of betrayal by NBC and Procter & Gamble.

CS fans went through similar disillusionment when producer Brian Park took the helm. Park killed off one too many of the characters viewers had got to know over the years; e-mail group posters wrote sadly about turning off their televisions and VCRs after years of watching *CS*.

Soap fans are perhaps the most loyal viewers of television programs, but even they have their limits. And they have long memories. They can recall story details from fifteen years back, and they can remember the head writer or producer who caused them to stop watching their story. That is something writers and producers would be well advised to remember, as is Carolyn Reynold's motto during her days as *CS* producer: If it ain't broke, don't fix it (Reynolds, interview).

Four
The Art of the Soaps II: Actors, Characters, and Stories

*Y*ou *have to breathe life into a character. Acting is acting; doesn't matter
if it's prime-time, movie of the week, stage, if you can't make a
character come alive, you shouldn't be an actor.*

LINDA DANO, FELICIA GALLANT ON AW (INTERVIEW)

As well as good stories, good acting makes for good soaps. But soaps more
than any other dramatic genre are beset by factors hostile to performance.
In the US in particular, soaps are not valued by the entertainment industry.
There is, therefore, no prestige for their actors outside soap opera circles,
and correspondingly little inducement for talented and ambitious actors to
consider soap roles worth vying for. But their lowly status is only one factor among a host of others that cast a pall over performance on American
soap operas.

Acting in American Soaps

Although critics often bemoan the clumsiness of the acting to be found in
soaps, they fail to ask why the acting is so often inept. Undeniably the quality of that acting varies—as it does in other dramatic genres—from individual to individual and over time. And lack of dramatic expertise on the part
of actors often does contribute to the poor quality of acting found in soaps.
But the line of questioning shouldn't end here: *why* is there this lack of
expertise?

Conventional wisdom has it that acting on soaps is bad because more
concern is taken with the looks of actors than with their ability.
Conventional wisdom in this case is partly correct: Jacqueline Brookes, a
New York stage actress and acting teacher who has extensive experience in
soap opera, confirms that in the early days actors were cast from modelling

agencies, not theatrical agencies (interview). But she adds that many contemporary soap actors, especially older and more established ones, have extensive training and experience. The late Douglass Watson (Mac Cory, *AW*), she remarks, was one of many actors, especially those based in New York, with extensive Shakespearean stage experience. Not infrequently, then, unevenness of performance cannot be pinned on lack of acting skill. To explain why soap acting sometimes disappoints, we need to look at a number of other factors.

Chief among these is time, in soaps a major constraint on even the best actor's ability to consistently deliver his or her best performance. Soap opera actors and writers commonly say that they create the equivalent of *two movies each week*, fifty-two weeks a year. Some rehearsal time is available, and retakes are now possible because all scenes are videotaped and then edited together. Things are not as harried as in the early days, when soaps aired live and then, in the 1970s, live to tape, and retakes were unthinkable. But even so, with an hour of programming airing each day, today's soaps find time for rehearsals and retakes extremely limited. And as Jacqueline Brookes says, "You are only as good as the material and the time you have to do it" (interview).

But the material as well can only be as good as time and other factors allow; in other words, the circumstances in which writers develop their stories and dialogue affect actors' ability to, as Linda Dano put it above, "breathe life" into their characters. And actors may be working with material that is less than a writer's best, again for lack of time.

In addition to time pressures, writers are also constrained in the stories they can tell by the demands of historical consistency; as we saw in the previous chapter, these demands can lie heavily upon them. Within these bounds, the stories told are also shaped by real life, which does not always cooperate with long-arc plot development. Changes are required by actor-related factors that may alter the plot direction as originally planned by the writers. These include the unexpected popularity of a character; the chemistry between actors, which may alter planned romantic pairings; an actor's decision to leave or return to a show; slipping ratings; real-life pregnancies; new production personnel; and even death: Mac Cory suffered a fatal heart attack while away from Bay City on a business trip soon after his portrayer, Douglass Watson, died.

Of all these, actor departures in general exert perhaps the greatest influence over plot direction. They can throw a spanner in the works, forcing new story directions and causing considerable plotline headaches for both writers and viewers, particularly when the departing actors are pivotal to the plot. Soaps, therefore, have developed a number of ways of handling this situation. To illustrate, let us look at perhaps the most popular soap partnership of all time, whose stars debuted *twice* in the same roles.

LUKE AND LAURA, SUPERCOUPLE

One of the most successful storylines in the short and long term in American soap history was the early 1980s action story of Luke and Laura on *GH*. The two were the creations of executive producer Gloria Monty. Ironically, in the beginning she did not intend them to be a couple. At the time of Luke's debut, Laura was already a well-liked character, paired with Scott Baldwin. Luke's incredible popularity among young viewers was unexpected; Monty's response was to pair him with Laura. Together the two were a phenomenal success, crossing boundaries to become celebrities in the mainstream entertainment industry. In the process they brought legitimacy to daytime serials. Lilana Novakovitch, Canadian agent for soap stars, credits them, and *GH*, with

> taking daytime out of the closet, so people were not ashamed to say "I watch a soap." *General Hospital* and Luke and Laura ... were like *the* super couple. They ended up being on the cover of *People* magazine, *Newsweek* magazine; they gave credibility to soap opera fans. (Interview)

What caused this interest? Lucas Lorenzo Spencer (played by Anthony Geary) was a young ne'er-do-well whose 1978 arrival in Port Charles led to long, multi-faceted stories about his involvement with, and subsequent defection from, mob boss Frank Smith. Tied in with this was his romance with young Laura Webber (Genie Francis).

In 1982 Francis left *GH*, followed in 1984 by Geary. Their absence was explained in this way: Luke and Laura were hiding from Frank Smith. Gloria Monty also left *GH* in 1984. In 1991 she returned to the serial, and soon after Geary returned to Port Charles, with his hair cut short and dyed red, in the character of Luke's cousin Bill Eckhart. Many in Port Charles commented on his resemblance to his cousin (although his appearance was considerably more altered than is often the case with dual roles). Like Luke, Bill was a good guy with an eye on the main chance and a willingness to walk close to the line of legality. His lower-middle-class family came with him, but did not remain in the lower ranks for long. Sister Jenny married millionaire Ned Ashton, but left Port Charles after they divorced. Mother left the family bakery for Europe, then briefly returned with a chic new look and job as a gallery owner's assistant. Bill stayed in Port Charles, where he was joined in 1993 by none other than Luke and Laura (as well as son Lucky), who had been running a diner in British Columbia while hiding out from Smith. Geary played a double role[50] until Bill was killed by a bullet intended for Luke.

Luke and Laura's return was a gamble on Monty's part; sometimes the magic is gone, especially when the pressure is on. Also, such high-profile "star" storylines may divert attention from other popular characters, alienating viewers who like those characters better. In this case things were handled skilfully:

> [The Luke-and-Laura] storylines have incorporated all of the cast, rather than alienating them.... If anyone out there was skeptical over whether the show could recapture the Luke and Laura magic 10 years later, they should have been ... Instead of attempting to recapture the magic, *GH* took this duo in new and exciting directions and let the magic take care of itself. (*SOD*, February 8, 1994: 17)[51]

Luke and Laura have since left and returned to Port Charles repeatedly as the actors portraying them have also done: Geary and Francis both left the show in December 1996. Their departure on screen was literally explosive: Laura was blown to pieces by a bomb detonated in a building, and Luke left with his son and baby daughter to return to the life of a drifter. But viewers were quickly reassured, through flashbacks, that Laura was, in fact, alive and the "explosion" was engineered by Luke and an accomplice, after she had left the building, to throw a family enemy off their track. This gave a plausible reason should the actors/characters return. Indeed, since then, Luke has returned and Laura has been in Port Charles for brief or longer stays. Francis's maternity leave and family life have led to Laura's periodic need to seek refuge elsewhere.

Through this brief history we can trace the way that the actors, the roles, and the script intersect and influence each other (responses to Luke's unexpected appeal and to the chemistry between Geary and Francis[52]), ultimately sculpting the contours of the characters viewers see on their screens. We can also see a couple of favoured tactics for dealing with the vagaries of actors' comings and goings: writing actors out (in hiding; killed in a blast); recasting as another character (cousin Eckhart); return to the original role, with explanation (out of hiding). All of these, of course, involve risks; all can be accomplished with greater or lesser finesse and can be ruinous if handled clumsily or with little regard for the audience's sensibilities.

An interesting resolution of a long-standing plotline dilemma about Luke and Laura's romance played out in the summer of 1998. Luke and Laura's first "date" many years ago ended in rape. But, due to Geary's great popularity with fans despite this, his character was redeemed, and the date rape was whitewashed. "Redemption" of rapists (or other villains) who turn out to be very popular characters/actors is not uncommon on soaps. What is uncommon is revisiting the crime, especially so many years later when only die-hard fans even know about it. However this happened with Luke and Laura. A teenage girl, Elizabeth, being attacked and raped in a public park provided the opportunity to explore the Spencer's personal history. Their son Lucky helped Elizabeth deal with the trauma of her rape, and in the course of that learned the truth about his parents. All parties had to deal with guilt and forgiveness, with what is reconcilable, and what is not, and why. It was a storyline which contrasted two situations involving two generations, explored the complexities of emotion and violation, and also wrapped up a long-existing loose end.

Recasting

One strategy obviously missing from the above account is recasting. There are some circumstances in which a character cannot be written out: if he or she is intrinsic to future story arcs, for instance, or if the actor departs in the middle of a storyline. In such cases, in American soaps a new actor is cast in the part. Recasting in general is unpopular with actors and audiences. Viewers come to "know" a character as he or she is portrayed by a particular actor, and changing that person necessarily must cause a change in the character. Writers and producers should be judicious in their decision to recast or write out a character. In cases such as Anthony Geary's Luke, recasting could not be an option, for some characters become so closely associated with the actors portraying them that recasts would almost certainly be rejected by viewers. Another such case occurred when Douglass Watson, who played Mac Cory on *AW*, died. According to one commentator, after Watson's death writers probably had little choice but to do Mac in: "[Watson] had made the part so much his own, they couldn't suddenly bring another guy in" (Brookes, interview).[53]

Understandably, actors would like to be irreplaceable. Jay Hammer, when he played Fletcher Reade on *GL*, spoke for his profession when he said, tongue-in-cheek, that if he left his role he hoped it would not be recast: "I hope I have left such an indelible impression on the character that [the writers] would feel chary about recasting the role for fear of audience revolt!" (interview).[54] But not all actors are intimately identified with their characters, at least not in the public's view; in these circumstances writers take less of a risk in resorting to a recast, weighing the gains in continuity of character and, to a great extent, storyline that a recast allows against the jolt to viewers and actors of writing a character out. Recasts can be tough on actors as well as viewers. Other actors must adjust to a new person while appearing to the audience to have the same relationship with the new as with the former actor. And the new actor must step into an already existing role, into a character whose personality bears the stamp, the personality and vision, of the person who previously had the role.

The least problematic recasts, at least for viewers, are short-term ones:

those that are temporary, the result of illness or family emergency. Because such situations generally cannot be anticipated and, therefore, cannot be provided for within the story, the recast is usually explained to viewers via a voice-over saying, "The role of so-and-so is being played temporarily by ..." The same type of announcement is sometimes used for permanent recasts, although conversational tags to aid viewer recognition of characters are also worked into the script. For instance, when a new actor first appears on screen, another person in that scene will say something like "Oh, _____, when did you come in?" This alerts viewers to the fact that the character now has a different face. (Of course, fans who buy industry magazines or visit internet groups or websites will have known of upcoming recasts months in advance.)

The ease with which a long-term recast "takes hold" is also affected by the way it is done. Recasts can be introduced abruptly, from one day to the next, or less jarringly, as when the character lies low for an interval before reappearing in a different guise; such changes may or may not be accompanied by storyline explanation—which can be more or less plausible. Those in the industry disagree on which strategy, sudden or gradual, is in the end less disruptive. Jacqueline Brookes, for instance, describes a recast that occurred when she was working on *Love of Life*:

> On her wedding day, they had [the original actress] go up to the altar with her back to the audience.... The last shot was her and her fiance.... The next day [the newlyweds] turned around: it was another actress! Well, of course, it caused huge outrage, but I think ... that's the best way. Outrage them and get it over with. (Interview)

Jay Hammer disagrees, seeing such abrupt change as too brutal on audiences and actors: he believes that it is better to let the character disappear for a while before returning in the form of a new actor (interview).

The details of a 1991 recast on *DOOL*—the reshuffling of storylines it occasioned—aptly illustrate the perils of recasting. The return of Deirdre Hall and Wayne Northrup to their roles as Dr. Marlena Evans and on-screen husband Roman Brady played havoc with actors and stories. Other actors were let go or back-burnered in order to showcase Hall and Northrup, who received star billing in the credits, something rare on soaps.[55] And the reintroduction of Hall and Northrup severely strained viewers' ability to suspend disbelief (this viewer's snapped).

Wayne Northrup, who played police commander Roman Brady, left *DOOL* in 1984; two years later Drake Hogestyn replaced him in the same role with the same name. Viewers and the residents of Salem accepted the fact that Roman now looked completely different. But in 1991 Northrup returned to the show, not as Roman's cousin or a long-lost "evil twin," but as Roman Brady himself, the "real" Roman, or Roman One as his family called him to distinguish him from Hogestyn's "Roman Two." Months passed while the Brady family tried to sort out why a man who bore no resemblance to Roman had so easily passed as him, fooling even Roman's mother. This might seem a difficult thing to explain, but soap writers certainly gave it a try: it all came back to the evil Stefano DiMera,[56] resident villain. Hogestyn, the bogus Roman, became known as "John Black," a man who had been tortured and brainwashed by Stefano who implanted the memories of the real Roman in his brain. This explained why John Black believed he was Roman Brady—but not why everyone else in Salem, including Brady's parents, wife, and children, did. The soap equivalent of Hamburger Helper, plastic surgery, was trotted out, but it really cannot explain differences in height and body build.

But more malevolent forces than Stefano DiMera were afoot in Salem. Strange, inexplicable things began happening in the town. Salemites, and viewers, at first assumed these were somehow Stefano's doing, but as disquiet deepened, they realized, with dawning horror, that someone still darker was responsible: the devil himself.

Behind the appearance of the devil we see the ingenuity of the writers at work. When Northrup again left the show in 1994, writers devised an over-the-top dramatic plotline: over many long months until mid-1995, Roman's ex-wife (and John Black's lover) Marlena Evans, a psychiatrist, was possessed by the devil. And Stefano was associated, in the minds of Salemites and therefore the audience, with this demonic force. Stefano had ruined Marlena's life and the lives of all those affected by the Roman Brady/John Black switch. The spiritual well-being of Marlena and all Salemites was endangered by the devil (read: Stefano's evil spirit). Note the link-up between the two major storylines, Brady/Black's and Marlena's: John, who after accepting that he was not Roman Brady, learned that he had been a Roman Catholic priest in the previous life he had not been able to remember and performed the exorcism of the demon that plagued Marlena.

While such an outrageous plot hook as demonic possession could not fail to raise eyebrows and excite viewer interest, the *DOOL* storyline went beyond this: it entered everyday discourse, even for people who had never watched the show. That, of course, was head writer James Reilly's intent:

> I spoke to so many people who said, "I heard about the devil story-line—that there was someone with crazy eyes, flying around. So I tuned in to see what was going on." They tuned in, and got hooked on Bo/Hope ... —which was the whole purpose. (*SOD*, February 13, 1996: 26)

The demonic element apparently so captured the public imagination that, a student told me, a man called a St. John's radio open-line show to ask, "Who is this Marlena, and why is she possessed by the devil?" This tale may be apocryphal, but even so it is a potent illustration of how deeply soaps have penetrated our awareness. The widespread familiarity with Marlena's plight attests partly to our fascination with such religious arcana as demonic possession, but it also signals the entrenchment of soaps in our society.[57]

In mid-1997 DOOL brought back the devil and Roman, though in very different ways. Stefano appeared sporting devil's horns as a comedic device in a campy storyline involving a rather deluded country girl, Susan (one of several roles played by Eileen Davidson),[58] who believed her son was fathered by Elvis Presley. Of course, the Elvis in the white-sequined cape who artificially inseminated her (shades of Dracula perhaps?) was none other than Stefano himself. When Susan learned how "evil, evil, evil" Stefano was, and that he, disguised as Elvis, had fathered her child, she had nightmares in which Stefano appeared not only as the devil, but claiming the loyalty of his devil spawn, her beloved son.

When Roman again returned from the "dead," looking totally different from the "real" Roman (as portrayed by Wayne Northrup),[59] no one in Salem batted an eyelid at the change in his appearance. But e-mail fans did. The new Roman, Josh Taylor, had previously played another character on DOOL, and the many long-time fans who remembered Taylor in that earlier role saw this casting choice as an insult to their intelligence (or at least their long-term memory) and their loyalty to the show.

When a role is recast, attention is usually paid to physical similarities. This may produce good or bad results. When Melissa Reeves was replaced as Jennifer on DOOL by Stephanie Cameron, who bears a striking resemblance to her, it took me several days, watching with only half my attention, to realize the person onscreen was not Reeves on a bad acting day. A successful recast was Brenda Epperson, who played Ashley Abbot on Y&R from 1988 to 1996. Epperson was hired despite her complete lack of acting experience because of her remarkable resemblance to her predecessor, Eileen Davidson, who later introduced the character of Kristen on DOOL. Physical similarity and the ability to move naturally on screen made for an easy and credible transition.

Sometimes, however, the new actor is nothing like the person he or she is replacing. A striking example is the 1993 recast of the character of Amanda Cory on AW. For the duration of Amanda's adolescence and early adult years[60] she was portrayed by Sandra Reinhardt, a pretty blonde of the young Doris Day type. Reinhardt was replaced in 1993 by Christine Tucci, a classically beautiful Joan Crawford-type brunette. The new Amanda was increasingly relegated to the background of storylines and eventually was sent off to live in Los Angeles. The writing out of a long-time major character sent a shockwave through the industry: "People are saying that if [*AW* executives] can get rid of Amanda Cory, they can get rid of anybody" (Tucci quoted in *SOD*, July 4, 1995: 7). Was it because the new Amanda, portrayed by a perfectly adequate actress, was not believable to viewers accustomed to Reinhardt? A red-haired Amanda returned to Bay City in December 1996, played by Laura Moss. She was replaced in April 1998 by blonde Sandra Reinhardt Ferguson: the "real" Amanda came home.

Writers may also recast when they decide to take a character in a different direction. *AW*'s Paulina Cory was originally played by Canada's Cali Timmins,[61] a delicate blonde. When the writers wanted to make Paulina a schemer with chutzpah, they decided the ethereal Timmins did not have the appropriate appearance. The new Paulina was Judi Evans Luciano, a more robust and sharper-edged woman who could match her then-romantic interest, Jake, in verbal and physical sparring. She changed the character and made it truly her own.

Another example is Carrie Brady on *DOOL*. When Carrie came back from her boarding school grown to young womanhood, she was first played by Christie Clark. Clark was replaced in 1992 by Tracy Middendorf, a quite ordinary-looking girl, who played Carrie as nasty and manipulative. But according to *DOOL* executive producer Ken Corday, the audience did not accept Middendorf in the character (or they didn't accept the character as played by Middendorf), so she was let go, and Christie Clark resumed the role (*SOD*, July 2, 1996: 49). Soon after Clark returned, Carrie became not only a more sympathetic character, but also won a fashion magazine cover-girl photo contest. (Carrie may have overcompensated for her past misdemeanours, however; she became so pure of heart—oblivious to her sister's incessant schemes to steal her fiancé—that she, and fiancé Austin, were nominated for *SOD*'s Dummy Awards for "most moronic moves" [*SOD*, April 9, 1996: 106]).

Despite the overall unpopularity ironically, recasting can in certain conditions actually be demanded by the audience. For example, e-mail soap fans howled for further recasting of two very unpopular *DOOL* actors, Austin Peck and Stephanie Cameron, immediately after they assumed their recast roles.

When Patrick Muldoon, who created the character of Austin Reed on *DOOL*, accepted an offer from the prime-time soap *Melrose Place* in 1995, he left Austin in the midst of a front-burner story—*DOOL* had little choice but to recast the role. Producers had six months' notice to find a new Austin, and they wrote the character out for an additional two months to ease the transition. But Muldoon's replacement, Austin Peck, bore little resemblance to Muldoon and had no previous acting experience (he'd been a model). Fans took savage note of the latter in e-mail discussions. The recasting of *DOOL*'s Jennifer after Melissa Reeves left her long-time (and very popular) role called forth a similar chorus of catcalls. The part of Jennifer had to be recast with no notice whatsoever (Reeves unexpectedly and very suddenly left the show because of personal circumstances); *DOOL*'s Ken Corday said they recast the part in *five days*. The new actress, Stephanie Cameron, had to immediately take over a very demanding work-load, with her character in the middle of a major storyline. The new Jennifer looks remarkably like the old, which Corday says is the best way to handle rushed recasts; he lets acting ability take second place to physical similarity in such cases (*SOD*, July 2, 1996: 47-8). According to fans, acting certainly took second place for both Cameron and Peck. The following exchange, from the discussion group *rats.misc*, May 9 and 10, 1996, was typical:

> B: Can anyone tell me if this actor [Austin Peck] has had any previous acting experience?... I can't decide if it's his hair or expressionless face.... His emotions seem so flat. I'm beginning not to care whether he ever gets Carrie back.

> S: Bwahahaha! Good one! By saying "previous acting experience" you are indicating that Austin is now or ever has acted. Well, heck no! What you're seeing is dialogue reading and the dear lad belongs with Jennifer, who is also a dialogue reader. They would bore each other into a coma and die and we *DOOL* fans would live happily ever after—until the next lame actor is hired.

No, soap fans do not just meekly accept whatever actor is slotted into a role.

GOINGS AND COMINGS

American soaps provide a valuable training ground for young actors who may work at different types of theatre, honing and expanding their skills, while they are employed on a soap or during times off. Cady McClain, Dixie on *AMC* until April 1996 and again in mid-1998, exemplifies the sort of drive that can benefit from the opportunities soap acting offers: "I trained the whole time I was [on *AMC*], took tons of classes and did lots of theatre. I wanted to become an actor who did a soap" (*SOD*, April 9, 1996: 17). Her co-star, acting veteran David Canary (Adam/Stuart), also stresses the impor-tance of learning the craft of acting before seeking stardom on stage or in film:

> Unfortunately many of these young kids just go from one television thing to another, hoping to get a movie. There's never any stage back-

ground or legit training ... it's like, "Gotta be relaxed, be cool" ... that's what they think is going to get them into films.... I don't *want* to be cool ... I want to act. (*SOD*, May 7, 1996: 36)

In addition to what Canary calls "legit" dramatic tutelage, soaps themselves can provide highly useful training: for neophyte actors, landing a job on a British or American serial is like jumping in the deep end. Even actors accustomed to the pace of television taping find the speed of soap production daunting. So soaps provide a good forum for actors to explore their craft, learn from their successes and failures, and discover how to make the best of the silliest of material. And in the very insecure world of acting, soaps can be a safe haven, although not all see that as necessarily good for an actor:

> The security of soap opera is seductive. I have tried to resist it—I am very grateful for the soap opera I have done and ... felt I got a lot from doing it... [It] can be quite creative if you don't do it for too long.... The security of it runs against the actor's grain in a way, and yet it is a very appealing thing ... [but] you get away from the theatre and the movies; it is very hard to do other things [at the same time] and also you don't have the energy after a while. (Brookes, interview)

Some, of course, successfully resist the siren's song of security, drawn instead to the lure of prime time and movies. Both novice and long-term soap actors often leave their roles to try their wings in Hollywood. They may succeed, as did Meg Ryan who found fame in the movie *When Harry Met Sally* after a two-year stint as Betsy on *ATWT* (see Butler 1995: 155–59). Others return to daytime for any number of professional or personal reasons. But all of these departures and returns must somehow be woven—more or less tightly—into the storyline. We have looked at a number of ways in which writers attempt to maintain or reintroduce a character; now let us consider how a character can be disposed of.

WRITING OUT

Sometimes an actor's reason for leaving a role is incorporated into the character's departure, creating a seamless fit between the two. When Michael Damian left *Y&R* to take up the lead in a Broadway production, so did his character, singer Danny Romalotti. Both returned to Genoa City afterward. Similarly, Ricky Paull Goldin left *AW* for a Broadway run in *Grease*, as did his character Dean Frame. Although Goldin, and Dean Frame, did not return to the soap, a journey by Joe Barbara (Joe Carlino, *AW*) to the same musical did end with his—and his character's—reappearance.

More commonly, however, characters who are written out move away or die. Killing off a character poses problems if writers or actors want the character to return—but nothing is impossible in the soaps: if you didn't see the corpse, the person isn't dead. Roger Thorpe on *GL*, when played by Michael Zaslow,[62] "died" twice. Speaking of his character's death and return to life, Zaslow told *SOD*:

> *Zaslow:* I insisted that he die. I did not want to do any more television, really, and knowing Roger was alive would have been too strong a temptation, because I had come back so many times.... But a decade later, needing a knee operation, having a child and knowing the knee operation would make me unemployable [in the theatre] for a year....
>
> *Digest:* When GL first approached you about coming back in 1989, didn't they ask you to play Alan? [a different and equally long-standing character who had an acrimonious relationship with Roger]
>
> *Zaslow:* Yeah. And I was deep in debt, and I really could have used the job, but I felt that to play a character that Roger was so involved with before would have been abusive to viewers. I said, "Well, if Roger were to make some miraculous entrance from the dead...." They said, "But he fell off a cliff!" Eventually, they viewed the tape and decided that he bounced. (*SOD*, July 4, 1995: 48, 51)

As well as highlighting an actor's need for economic security, Zaslow's story illustrates the sometimes cavalier attitude producers adopt towards actors, their characterizations, and, especially, their audiences. The back-from-the-dead device has been used often enough that, if it is done cleverly, it doesn't perturb viewers who may well be pleased to see favourite actors return. But coming back to a different role, as *GL* executives proposed to Zaslow, is rarely acceptable. An example is Nicolas Coster's return to *ATWT* as Eduardo Grimali, husband of Lisa, after having earlier played John Eldridge, her former husband. In response, an e-mail message joked: "Lisa has had so many husbands she doesn't realize she has duplicates" ("S," *rats.cbs*, May 14, 1996).

Jeremy Butler (1995) argues that fan willingness to accept recasts shows that actors are virtually interchangeable on American soaps and fans neither care nor notice. That may appear to be so, especially given the frequency of recasts and the number of actors who leave one soap only to pop up on another. Butler cites *GH*'s Geary and Francis (Luke and Laura) as examples: their departure "did no irreparable harm to its [*GH*'s] popularity—just as Geary's return to the program *as a different character* ... did not catapult it to the top of the ratings" (1995: 148; emphasis in text). However, Butler has failed to consider a key feature of viewer attachment to the soaps: soap fans are intensely loyal, first and foremost, to "their" stories. Moreover, they understand the industry. The contours of real and therefore screen lives can shift rapidly, without warning; soap fans accept these realities, but this does not mean they go unnoticed. For, even as its characters and plotlines shift and despite the loss of beloved actors and characters, *the story goes on.* Departing actors are wished well in future endeavours, but viewer allegiance does not centre on them. There are exceptions: some fans will start watching a new show if a favourite actor moves to it, but "stars" have not been a cornerstone of soaps for the industry or the viewers.

Respecting the fans

There is, in the convolutions of plots devised to ease recasts, reprisals of roles, and writings out, much potential for audience abuse, even aside from the insensitivity of the executive powers in the soap industry. What is perhaps notable is how many plots do work, how much inventiveness is brought to bear, and how high the success rate is. The low points do receive disproportionate attention; this is because they *grate.* And perhaps it's simply more fun to lampoon silliness. At any rate, there is certainly silliness to seize upon. *SOD* has even institutionalized that quality by annually conferring on some serial storyline the title "Most Preposterous Plot." In 1994 it reserved that honour for the explanation of the recasting of *AMC*'s psychotic murderer Janet Green:

> It's true that hardened criminals volunteer to be guinea pigs for medical experiments.... But All My Children went too far asking us to believe that the prison system would actually commute ... Janet Green's life sentence merely because she agreed to undergo an experimental face-lift.... Was she helping to eradicate crow's feet? (January 3, 1995: 33)

There really is no credible explanation for a total transformation in appearance, so perhaps no explanation should be proffered: writers should just rely on audience good will and willingness to suspend disbelief. But belief can only be suspended so far, even when popular actors return to roles in which they were killed off. Sometimes the explanations just do not work:

> Take [*DOOL'S*] Kristian Alfonso (Hope). Alfonso is one of daytime's
> most popular performers, but fans cried foul when it took Hope over
> a year to learn her real name [amnesia!]. (*SOD*, October 10, 1995:
> 100)[63]

Another tactic, the return of a popular actor for a brief period, must similarly be handled with due respect for the audience:

> The temptation to bring back popular actors for brief periods during
> sweeps weeks is strong, but gimmick returns can do more harm than
> good. Fans had been begging for [*GL's*] Kim Zimmer (Reva) to
> reprise her role, but that didn't mean they would accept her as a
> ghost. Ditto *General Hospital's* Jack Wagner (ex-Frisco), whose three
> comebacks (during successive sweeps periods) left fans feeling like
> Frisco had turned into a jerk.[64] (*SOD*, October 10, 1995: 100)

Fans know that popular actors are brought back for short-term appearances
during ratings periods. They also know what prevented an actor such as Jack
Wagner, a *GH* favourite as Frisco Jones, from returning on a long-term
basis: his role on *Melrose Place*. Nor could Frisco be recast: he was popular
enough as a character, as was Jack Wagner as his portrayer, that recasting
would not be acceptable to viewers. Nor was he integral to the storyline of
the time. His whirlwind returns amount to little more than glorified cameo
appearances; to long-time fans, who want continuity of character and story,
bringing him back briefly only annoys, and to new viewers his return may
only be confusing because they don't know his character's history in the
soap. It might be better just to consign him to what e-mail group fans call
"the black hole" or the "Bermuda Triangle" of unresolved soap stories.

Acting in British Serials

We have noted, in earlier chapters, that British soaps differ greatly in production methods and storyline philosophy from the American product. To
this list we can now add striking differences in acting and characterization.
It is useful to think of British production, as concerns acting, as precisely the
mirror image of American production.

In Britain, unlike in the US, serials air in prime time and are not viewed
as a degenerate genre. They are legitimate in themselves, rather than simply
stepping stones to stage or film roles. Hardly surprisingly, the quality of acting in British serials in general is consistently higher than that in American
ones. One reason for this is obvious: serials are more attractive to actors
because of their higher status, and so they attract better actors. A role on

CS, *EE*, or any of the other major British serials is a valuable item on the résumé of any actor; nothing remotely similar, as we saw, can be said for American soap roles.

A second, practical reason for the higher quality of acting on British serials is the frequency of programming. British serials are a half-hour in length and air at most four times weekly. There is simply more time than in American soaps for rehearsal and retakes in order to obtain the best possible performance.

Writers and producers also enjoy higher status and so produce to more exacting, though very different, standards. The approach to storytelling taken by British serial writers as against American writers is, as Tony Warren, Tom Elliot, and Carolyn Reynolds all told me, simply that British serials are *character*-driven whereas American soaps are *plot*-driven:

> I think the writing is extremely powerful on *Coronation Street*. It balances beautifully the northern humour ... with stories that are very strong emotional, character-led stories. They are always truthful to the character ... [Of] each character in *Coronation Street* you can probably say oh yes, I know someone who is like that.... You will always have conversations with writers saying I'm sorry, Jack Duckworth would not *do* this.... They are very specific about characters. And because it's very strong writing ... coupled with very good performances, actors have lived those characters for so long that they know them inside out. So you've got a wonderful harmony of two areas that are vital to the success of a long-running series. (Reynolds, interview)

What this focus means in concrete terms is that a character on a British serial rarely does something that doesn't ring true to his or her personality. Almost always, if a planned plotline calls for Jack Duckworth to do something not in his nature, the plot will be changed, not Jack. And if someone does do something uncharacteristic, it will be commented on by other people in the show, and some reason for the aberrant behaviour will out. On American soaps, as we have seen, characters may undergo complete personality or physical changes with no adequate explanation, or they act in ways jarringly inconsistent with their past history. Usually these character twists are intended to push the plotline in a new direction or to prolong an intrigue or mystery. In other words, integrity of characterization may be sacrificed to the story. This can impart to a storyline a strained quality that cannot help but infect the acting.

Examples from the same Canadian broadcast week of *CS* and *DOOL* nicely illustrate the British/American divide over consistency of characterization. November 28, 1995, saw the departure of Bet Gilroy (played by Julie

Goodyear) from the Rovers Return and *CS*. Proud and forthright, the proverbial "floozy with the heart of gold," Bet came to the Street in 1970, worked as a barmaid at the Rovers, and eventually became its manager. When the brewery that owned the pub decided to sell it, Bet tried to raise the money to buy it, but was unsuccessful. Her step-granddaughter, who inherited a considerable fortune by the death of her parents a few years earlier, refused to loan her the money, but offered to buy her a house "as a real estate investment." Bet reacted in perfect style. Flamboyant to the ends of her long polished fingernails and cigarette holder, in a grand gesture only she could pull off, she ordered her granddaughter out of the pub. She told the patrons that she had wanted to throw each and every one of them out at some point, and she was doing it now. After they hurriedly left, she locked the pub, packed her leopard-patterned suitcases, donned her leopard-skin coat and huge rhinestone earrings,[65] and left in a taxi for parts unknown. While her actions shocked audience and Street characters alike, the combination of hurt and pride with which Julie Goodyear imbued her performance was dramatically moving and consistent with the Bet familiar to all.

On the same day, on *DOOL*, John Black reacted to the accusation made by Tony DiMera that John was responsible for the gunshot wound from which Tony was dying. Tony hated him because Tony's wife Kristen had left him for John. Having learned that he had an unnamed, fatal blood disease, Tony kept his illness secret and began plotting his revenge. By rigging up an elaborate system using John's revolver and timing devices, he fatally shot himself from across a room after provoking a violent argument with John which everyone, including his ex-wife, heard. They also heard Tony being shot after pleading with John for mercy, although, unbeknown to them, John had already left the room. John had been saying for weeks that Tony was up to something; even during the argument he thought something was strange. Yet when he was found and informed that he was the prime suspect, he never mentioned these suspicions. He said things like, "Tony's not rational; when he comes around he'll clear this up." A precedent for this incident had been set by Tony's father Stefano, who also hates John and who faked his own death by blowing himself up in his car in full view of John, Kristen, and Tony. Like father, like son? John is, after all, on record saying that Tony would do anything to destroy him. Finally, during his tenure as police commander, John was regarded by all Salem as very intelligent and intuitive. Why can't he see that Tony could have created a very clever set-up? For the sake of a dramatic storyline, viewers are expected to believe in John's complete loss of common sense about his principal enemy. On the longer storyline arc, we are to accept that a "good" character, Tony, became so twisted with hatred that he would take a revenge that benefits no one, including himself.

Whereas American fans have learned to accept the disappearance or recasting of characters, British fans and producers identify the characters with their actors. It makes sense, then, that British soap actors are generally restricted by contract from taking other acting jobs in the UK. In the words of Elizabeth Dawn (Vera Duckworth on *CS*), "that's what makes the characters believable. I mean, they're a bit unbelievable, aren't they, if you see them [the actors] on other programs" (interview). On British serials, in general, actors become intimately connected with their characters and recasts are virtually non-existent.[66] A corollary of this organic fit between actor and character is that there is in Britain none of the kaleidoscopic shuffling of actors one sees on American soaps: characters are not written in and out with such abandon, for it is unlikely that an actor well known in a certain role could successfully adopt a new role on another show. Bill Tarmey, for instance, has been playing his character Jack on *CS* for twenty years now. He has not, of course, been playing him *in the same way* for twenty years: character-driven does not mean static. But it does mean the character changes in a relatively gradual, *realistic* way. After clarifying that his first appearances on *CS* were as an occasional extra in the Rovers Return, Tarmey says of his character Jack:

> When I first started playing [Jack] he was more aggressive than he is now. Then again, over fourteen years, he now works with females all the time and that would mellow any man.... There was a time when [real life] guys wanted to fight me at the bar and little old ladies used to smack me with handbags, but they don't any more. They just laugh. (Interview)

Tarmey muses on Jack's, and his own, future:

> [Jack] will get older. Unless of course because the production people deem it right, or the public, or myself, [to] kill him off. It's a possibility ... people say you're fixed [on *CS*] for life and all that; that is a lot of nonsense. You just do the job and don't look too far in the future. (Interview)

It is not likely that Jack will die unless Tarmey decides to leave the show. That is also somewhat unlikely: established actors like Tarmey and his co-star Elizabeth Dawn know that they have good roles that allow them to stretch their dramatic abilities and earn respect. And as in the US, serials provide valuable training. A young actor like Nicholas Cochrane (Andy McDonald), who was hired straight from secondary school, knew he had an opportunity for invaluable training (interview). British actors can and do take short-term leaves of absence from their shows. But the decision to leave permanently is a weightier one because it is irrevocable: all British serial actors know that if their character is killed off there are no returns from the dead.

Five
Spinning Dreams or Living Life: Messages of the Soaps

*F*rank Barlow to son Ken (while pouring ketchup on his meal): "What's that snooty expression for? Bet they don't do that at college, do they? (To wife) That lad should learn to live in his own class.... We certainly raised a rum 'un."
Albert Tatlock to Ken: "Never thought I'd say, that school's turned you into a proper little snob."

FIRST EPISODE OF CORONATION STREET, DECEMBER 1960

*N*ick to his father Victor Newman: "All built by one man! How did you do it?"
Victor: "Would you believe, I had no other option. You must remember, my boy, I grew up in an orphanage. That kind of stuff either puts you in a deep depression or is a hell of a motivator."

THE YOUNG & THE RESTLESS, ON THE CREATION OF
THE INDUSTRIAL EMPIRE NEWMAN ENTERPRISES (SPRING 1996)

SHOULD we think of the British and American soaps as no more than diversion or amusement, or are they instruments of instruction or social change?[67] Tony Warren, creator of *CS*, has firm opinions on this matter:

[*CS*] is purely and simply entertainment, and disposable entertainment at that. It was never designed to be anything more, or anything less, than that ... When it stops being that it worries me." (Interview)

Perhaps Warren should start worrying. For audiences, as well as being entertained, do glean messages about society and behaviour from the soaps they watch. The question is not *whether* soaps exert some influence over their audience, but *the nature* of the influence they exert. Precisely *what* do the soaps say to us, and *how*?

We need to approach this question with some delicacy, for it is a complex one and has attracted a great deal of empirical research, unfortunately without generating much consensus on how media in general influence our thoughts and behaviour. I will not venture into the empirical studies (the interested reader should consult communications studies and psychology journals), but will attempt to clarify the question itself, to sort out the various ways in which we might understand the alleged influence of soaps.

We often speak as though the soaps, or any other form of media, have one monolithic, determinate message to impart. We have no reason to assume this, and every reason not to. Consider the intricacy of much smaller units of communication, for example words, and how they function in language: multifaceted to begin with, varying and flowing in sense with the smallest shift in context or nuance. Against this, a vehicle employing linguistic, visual, and auditory elements of meaning might well take on great complexity. What sort of message or messages is it that soaps supposedly convey? Having answered this, we can then inquire into their content.

The soap industry and its advertisers must have long believed that people gather information during the shows. These ads apprise viewers of the availability and uses of various products.[68] Soaps themselves, analogously, deliver straightforward information about how things are done, from how others handle emotional crises to how one arranges a garden wedding. *CS*, for instance, "educates" by accident: years ago, when Stan and Hilda Ogden were the Street's somewhat ne'er-do-well couple, Bernard Youens, who played Stan, became ill. In order to explain his absence, the writers put Stan to bed. In the storyline, he injured his toe on a sidewalk brick and was laid up, occasionally knocking on the floor for Hilda to bring him a cup of tea.

> Someone discovered that if a paving stone is sticking up over a certain amount ... you have a claim against the council. So Hilda went to a solicitor and sued the council, and she got paid.... And councils were up in arms against *Coronation Street* because claims against them for tripping over paving stones that were over three-quarters of an inch high went up 200 per cent... We had a good tale, it's the story, the characters ... and what we actually did was educate the public! (Elliot, interview)

In a 1992 storyline, unemployed Martin Platt enrolled in nursing school. The story purpose was to put his marriage in jeopardy, as Martin would now be surrounded by nubile young women. But it also prompted a sharp increase in inquiries to nursing schools from men (Elliot and Reynolds, interviews). Clearly, soaps do communicate information, and they do have an impact, intentional or not, on viewers.

Nor has that impact always been entirely accidental. This might be thought unsurprising in the British context, where radio serials were explicitly designed as educational tools (see chapter one). But the informative potential of American soaps has also been noted and utilized when it was thought expedient, notably during the Second World War. Carol Williams writes:

> The War Department wanted soap opera to teach its huge audience how to react to death, for reaction, more than action, is the subject matter of soaps. The government also hoped the serials would temper racism because it believed "conservative whites" were "amongst the most fervent addicts of soap operas." Hence, for example, a story in which Helen Trent was saved by a black doctor: "Helen's gratitude stretched over several weeks, and gave rise to many a discussion of black patriotism, blacks' qualities and capabilities, and their patience in the face of white persecution." (Williams 1992: 20–21, citing P. Buckman 1984: 20-21, 22)

There are also what Williams calls "the 'public service' stories on breast cancer, addiction, or abuse" (1992:96) that deal with a social or medical issue about which most viewers would agree that public awareness should be increased. They provide information on treatments for diseases or addictions, as well as information, for example, on how to leave abusive relationships or enrol in adult literacy classes. Other, more controversial issues are also presented, ones that viewers may not think suitable as light entertainment viewing material. Abortion, AIDS, and homosexuality are examples of topics that have generated mixed audience response when they've been part of soap stories. The number of these "teaching" and "issue" storylines presented on American soaps has increased in recent years, with each serial usually having at least one socially relevant plot on the go at any given time.

There is a certain pressure to include such stories, though that pressure lands soap writers and sponsors, especially in the US, in a creative conundrum. The last thing they want to do is alienate viewers by presenting controversial issues; yet in order to tell effective stories, stories that will catch their audience's interest, they must deal with matters that are part of that audience's realities.[69] The result is an uneasy balance, with the soaps sometimes ahead of prime-time television programming in presenting topical issues and sometimes behind. For instance, *AW* had an illegal abortion in 1965 and *AMC* featured the first legal abortion on television in 1971 (Williams 1992: 98), well before other television programming was willing to deal with it. Other issues were later in coming to soaps, and were couched more tentatively, interracial relationships, homosexuality, and political realities among them. Even Agnes Nixon, *OLTL* writer extraordinaire who was greatly committed to presenting stories about real issues in American society, did not want to push viewers too far. In 1987, asked when she planned to run an AIDS story, she replied that "she did not think the audience was ready. 'It's all you people in the Midwest,'" she joked with her interviewer (Williams, 1992: 94). Yet by 1987 the enormity of the AIDS threat was hardly news, presumably not even in Peoria.

In general, no one on either end of the political spectrum can defend spousal abuse or irresponsible teenage sex; therefore those kinds of stories are relatively safe and easy to present. Story themes on which the populace has strong and divided opinions are treated more circumspectly[70] than "mainstream" stories related to sexual activity and physical health. AIDS, homosexuality, and poverty are harder to deal with without offending some part of the viewing audience. Among the touchiest of issues are political ones. Agnes Nixon again has been the boldest in tackling such matters.

A storyline that Nixon introduced into *AMC* in 1970 was, according to one writer, the "first and only time" a current political issue was included in soap opera. The subject was the Vietnam War. "The speech against the war at that time by [a mother whose son was missing in action in Vietnam] ... was noted on political pages: Even the mothers on those escapist soap operas were against the war, it was said" (Williams 1992: 99-100). Thereafter, the Vietnam War did not return to soaps until the middle and late 1980s, and again soon after the 1991 Gulf War (when Dr. John Hudson of *AW* helped a Gulf War veteran deal with his trauma by sharing his own memories of the earlier conflict). But by the 1980s, of course, the Vietnam War was no longer a delicate topic. The general rule is clear: political issues have no place in the world of soaps.[71]

AIDS provides another interesting test case. Despite its prevalence among the male homosexual population of North America, the disease has only once, to my knowledge, directly concerned a gay man on an American soap: on *OLTL* in 1992 (see Fuqua 1995). On soaps the HIV virus is usually contracted by a woman from a man, both of whom are usually tangential characters in whom viewers have little emotional investment.[72] Transmission usually involves, perhaps at some remove, illicit behaviour. (*Y&R*'s Jessica contracted it when she was working as a prostitute; *AW*'s Dawn through a blood transfusion from her mother, a prostitute; *AMC*'s Cindy from her husband, a drug addict.) Industry personnel justify this focus on heterosexual AIDS and women as a way of not ghettoizing the disease:

Soap makers argue that their audience is women and will identify with women characters. There may be wisdom here. Soaps are the genre for getting to know people, and perhaps mass America will do better getting to know people with AIDS without at first adding drug addiction or homosexuality.... [But] in linking AIDS with women, victimization, and immorality, daytime drama subtly debases both women and the disease. (Williams 1992:113)

Another researcher sees the use of marginal characters in potentially controversial storylines as a way of protecting the shows, of not risking offending parts of their audience. Fuqua (1995: 201-2) suggests that using marginal characters to present contentious issues allows "the teaching of 'tolerance' of [differences of] race, class, and recently, sexuality" at minimal risk to sponsors and the soaps themselves. Alan Filewod, professor of drama at Guelph University, agrees. He argues that in general, soaps succeed in "circulating social issues" and presenting them in personal terms rather than as systemic in society.

> They're not actually addressing the sources of the problems ... the social forces that define the problem [and] the social conditions that keep these problems going.... They're basically turning them into gossip ...
>
> To examine an issue means to interrogate its sources, to look at how it is formed in society and the social factors that cause it and shape it.... They do not look at the sources of racism, do not look at the complex issues behind a question like abortion. They put them in terms of simple personal dilemmas that have to be worked out in order to keep the plot moving. (Interview).

Yet another concern for soap writers is integrity of character, which is essential to all good story-telling. What happens to characters will be believable and effective only if the event, and their reactions to it, fit their nature; topical social issues, if imposed on unlikely characters, violate continuity of character and story. The British practice of letting character lead plot means, usually, that even stories dealing primarily with social issues flow smoothly in keeping with character. It is the type of storytelling about which Carolyn Reynolds says:

> We know of other long-running [British] drama serials [where] a producer will ... say, "I want an AIDS story." We would never do that because we prefer to look at characters and say, "We need a story for Curly, or we need a story for Angie." We would never say, "We want an AIDS story." We would do it in reverse. (Interview)

The power of soaps to effectively convey information through story has not been lost on social agencies and activist groups, many of which petition the soaps to work their causes into their storylines. Carolyn Reynolds, when she was producer of *CS*, avoided doing so:

> We ... always said we're not a public service, we're not a documen-tary.... We are a drama series.... I think you can certainly heavily influence people. There [was] a great temptation, I must admit. I'm very keen on protecting the environment, green issues, and I [had] to smack myself every now and then and stop me from doing a story about it. (Interview)[73]

There is yet another, more subtle, sense in which soaps can be considered instructive. Since they concentrate on interpersonal relations—romance, family, friendship—set in a social and political milieu intended to parallel the surrounding society, they can hardly fail to send messages about appro-priate or expected behaviour. That is, they take on a normative hue; the very act of presenting and attending to certain behaviours and events rather than others showcases or "privileges" the ones selected, for television is above all a medium of glamour.

Some critics argue that the soaps' great reliance on infidelity, intrigue, lying, and promiscuous sex tacitly legitimizes such behaviour, exerting a subtly corrupting influence on impressionable young viewers.[74] This criti-cism has three components: (1) soaps contain a great number of scenes depicting immoral behaviour; (2) this behaviour is portrayed as in some sense acceptable and is therefore "endorsed"; (3) such depictions adversely influence susceptible members of the audience. The third claim is a highly contentious one, subject of much complicated yet still inconclusive research; fortunately, we need not become entangled in its tentacles, for I see the argument as breaking down long before it arrives there.

Indisputably, the first claim is true: soaps contain many scenes depicting various shades of sleazy behaviour. Indeed, loose goings-on could be said to be the engine driving soap storylines. Even on *CS*, where I know of very few explicit sexual scenes, high-school teacher Ken Barlow as of 1995 had a "bed count" of twenty-three, including three wives (*Yes! Magazine*, September 17, 1995: 8). The raw numbers speak for themselves; but as we noted in chapter one, they don't tell the whole story. We also need to con-sider *context*, the broader storyline in which the incidents are embedded. This is where those who see soaps as glamourizing adultery and deceit reveal themselves as not terribly familiar with their subject, for, as Al Rosenberg of *Daytime TV* explains, soaps are:

like a morality play. Anybody who does anything wrong usually pays for it. If a teenager has sexual relations for the first time, she's going to get pregnant—one time!.... and she's going to have to face the consequences ... this, in effect, teaches youngsters: hey, if you fool around with something that you can't control, you're going to pay the price later on. (Interview)

The theme of punishment, or come-uppance, for bad choices has always run through soap plots. For example, consider this storyline introduced on *AMC* in late 1995: a teenaged runaway, Kelsey, turns up in Pine Valley's homeless shelter, pregnant from her first and only sexual encounter. She had tried to get an abortion, but had waited too long. Although unhappy about her pregnancy, she believed the father of her baby loved her; if she could find him, all would be fine. When she discovered him with her friend, he had no recollection of ever meeting her, saying in fact that he had been blind drunk on the night in question. She did not tell him about the baby until she realized he was putting pressure on Anita to "prove her love" through sex. Kelsey launched a double-sided campaign: she will tell Anita that the baby is his if he does not stop his seduction efforts, and she straightforwardly tells Anita what can result from falling for boys' lines.

The message in this case was presented with a light hand and, what is invaluable in solidifying new roles, Kelsey was linked to other principal characters: although she grew up in Oregon, she was the granddaughter of Dr. Joe Martin, whose family has been central to *AMC* since its inception. Moreover, Anita's sister Maria and her husband, who had been unsuccessfully attempting *in vitro* fertilization, arranged to adopt Kelsey's baby. The important point is that Kelsey's story is hardly one of cavalier, casual sex without consequence.

After Kelsey arrived on the scene, teenage sex and family relations were further explored. Maria confronted her authoritarian father after he publicly and wrongly accused her sister Anita of sexual activity, revealing that she herself had not been as perfect as he believed; she had got pregnant when a teenager and been afraid to tell her parents. She miscarried but, due to fear and shame, did not see a doctor. An untreated infection damaged her fallopian tubes, causing her infertility. So, the lessons to young people are clear: 1. don't fool around and 2. be honest with your parents; and, to parents, give your children the room to be honest. (The only surprising oversight was the apparent lack of condom use. It is now commonplace for "protection" to be mentioned, and for AIDS tests to follow in cases where they are not used.)

Another source of criticism is the way in which soaps "feed off" familial conflict. Soap marriages, in particular American ones, are rarely stable. Producers see happily married couples as boring; front-burner stories are believed to come from passionate union quickly followed by betrayal and separation. Tellingly, in a profile of a "loving" couple, *Soap Opera Update* wrote:

> And the two have been revelling in their newfound happiness ever since. "He loves me!"... and as she whirled around, grinning from ear to ear, we smiled back.
> But as we are talking about a soap opera, we must remember that no couple can experience smooth sailing for more than a day or two. (Feb. 8, 1994: 51)

Many soap actors dread the day their character gets married because after the honeymoon, the couple will likely have at least a brief period of untroubled bliss, for the duration of which their actors can expect little airtime. And if they stay married, their storylines are further back-burnered.[75] This is seen as an unfortunate unreality by some. Actors Maureen Garrett and Michael Zaslow discussed the likelihood of their *GL* characters remarrying:

> *Garrett:* ... we were looking forward to playing Holly and Roger in a healthy, mature, give-and-take relationship. The powers-that-be did not find that dramatically interesting ...
>
> *SOD:* Producers think that a happy couple is a boring couple.
>
> *Zaslow:* But what is "happy," anyway? If I think about my relationship with my wife over the last 20 years—we weren't always happy. We fought, we loved, we worked. It is happy, ultimately, from some long perspective, but it's not without drama, let me tell you. (*SOD*, July 4, 1995: 47)

But day-to-day marital problems are not deemed gripping enough to sustain viewer interest. A reasonably functional marriage typically means the end of a frontburner storyline for actors;[76] something "big" has to happen to maintain dramatic tension in the marriage. That something is usually adultery, work pressures, or the unearthing of a damaging secret, such as an illegitimate child or substance abuse or addiction.[77]

British serials, however, have longer-lasting marriages and find much of the drama of their stories in the day-to-day lives of couples, in their relationships with each other and the community.

In the soaps of both countries, characters aspire to the ideal of happy and stable marriages. This is shown both in the dialogue between partners and in the advice given women and men by friends and family. So, despite the adultery and duplicity, the underlying values promoted are exactly the opposite of deceitful, both implicitly—through the negative consequences attached to underhand dealings—and explicitly—through dialogue and the positive consequences of honesty.

Messages concerning emotional relationships are made specific in instructional ways only when unforeseen physical consequences result, such as unwanted pregnancy or sexually transmitted disease. Otherwise, messages concerning appropriate or inappropriate behaviour are embedded in the dramatic structure. Soaps, after all, are primarily about the domestic and emotional realms. And both these realms can be explored within a larger, social context.

The Social Geography of Soaps

Soap stories of romance and family, like real-life ones, are located within a wider world of community, work, and societal concerns. But the emphasis on social and work worlds differs radically in the two countries.

Community enters into American soaps in two ways. One is the result of intertwining storylines of family and romance: friendships are part of life and therefore are reflected in the naturalistic cast of storytelling in American soaps. They also serve to link separate plots and characters, as a romance or argument can later be discussed with another soap character, adding another layer of narrative and giving a different perspective.

Community can also form the basis of plotlines only tangentially concerned with romance. Neighbourhood development in conflict with industry was the issue in a 1994 *GH* story that involved many existing characters and introduced a new family, the Wards, a family committed to social justice issues through community, family, and legal venues. In American soaps, "community issue" stories address some present-day social reality. In this case the Quartermaine company wanted to locate a waste facility near a run-down part of town in which the Wards and Spencers lived. Laura Spencer and the Wards mounted a lobby campaign that defeated the proposed industry.

In the tradition of linking new characters to existing families through romance or kinship, both Wards and Quartermaines learned of connections known only by the Ward family matriarch, Mary Mae Ward (bear in mind the Wards had never appeared on *GH* prior to this). The twenty-year-old mystery of the disappearance of Mary Mae's son, a social-activist politician, was solved. He had been murdered in the interests of industrial development by Edward Quartermaine's cronies. When suspicion fell on Edward, Mary Mae confessed that Edward was her deceased son's father; he had had an affair with her when she was a young jazz singer, but he never knew she had become pregnant. So the two families, on opposite sides of the political fence (and, rather daringly for soaps, one white and one black family), were related. Romance sprang up between a young Quartermaine and a (non-kin) Ward, completing the soap opera formula of intermeshed community issues, history, kinship, and romance. The son of Mary Mae's murdered son became part of his grandfather Edward's business empire and eventually took his full place in the dysfunctional family life of the Quartermaine clan.

Such interweaving of specific neighbourhoods through community bonds, however, is relatively rare on American daytime. Most American serials have a seedy part of town, but it is invoked only to further other stories. In 1995, *AMC*'s Erica Kane, glamorous and wealthy television celebrity, survived a trip to dangerous Front Street to find a drug dealer to sell her the pain-killers to which she was addicted. Earlier, middle-class Julia fled to Front Street to get away from her family. She was taken in by a street tough (Noah, who subsequently fell in love with her), raped by a drug dealer, became pregnant, and, over her Roman Catholic family's objections and those of anti-abortion activists, had an abortion. But throughout all this, viewers got no sense of the community of Front Street because it was there simply as a prop for action, a backdrop for the activity of "respectable" characters. If the residents of such communities stay in the storyline, they leave the slums, as did Julia's lover, Noah, and Stone of *GH*.[78]

Nor are the middle-class and affluent neighbourhoods of major characters shown. References to urban geography are infrequent; only rarely can we discern the proximity of friends' houses, or who the neighbours are. Even the community-minded Laura Spencer is not seen visiting with her next-door neighbour. The important "community" is maintained through family, friends, and workplace, not physical proximity.

In British serials, by contrast, family and neighbours are the bedrocks on which the stories take place. Actual streets, whether outdoor studio backlot sets or *Brookside*'s housing estate, certainly help to establish this sense of identifiable community, but are not strictly necessary. Long before *CS*'s outdoor street set was built, street-front facades conveyed the sense of who lived where on the street and who lived nearby. Neighbourhood also comes through in the type of stories told and in the manner of telling: newcomers and outsiders are kept at a distance until they are more of a known quantity. The only unexplained and ignored outsiders are the extras who fill the Rovers Return; but a pub does need more patrons to stay afloat than one block-long street can provide. No one ever talks to the extras, but we know that is a matter of acting contracts and pay rates. (Suspension of disbelief does have to be employed with British serials as with American, just not to the same extent.)

Another reason for the prominence of neighbourhood in British serials is the pre-eminence of place, both social and geographical, in British society. British soaps are more rooted in history, both of the program itself and the social reality it presents. Change is slow to occur and not necessarily seen as good; what is important is to stick together with one's own people and one's own ways.

It is interesting to refract these differences through the prism of interior/exterior, physical and mental space. American soaps are about interiors: the emotions of characters and the appeal to the viewer's feelings. In general, we watch not so much to see *what* characters are doing as how they *feel* about what they are doing. We often hear their thoughts, for instance through a voice-over during a close-up facial shot. As if to buttress this "inner-directness," the action of American soaps takes place indoors. I am familiar with the inside of several rooms in many houses, but have no idea what the outsides look like. *AMC* occasionally shows shots of the exteriors of the Marick and Cortlandt mansions, but they are not incorporated into the story; they are just shots of the types of manors we pay money to tour while dreaming of owning such opulence. (True, American soaps also rely on room interiors because they are produced inside studios; pragmatic and conceptual demands coincide.) That American soaps explore the interior contours of emotional life is the product of their roots in melodrama, which is all about heightened emotionalism, compared to the British tradition of social realism.

British serials are about exteriors; they deal as much with community interaction as they do with the emotional content of relationships. Even within a relationship, viewers see as much about how the partners feel about other people or their work as they do about each other. And much of the action takes place outdoors or in public sites like workplaces or the pub.

Contrast, for instance, the way wife abuse was dealt with on *CS* compared to *Y&R*. The beating of April on *Y&R* took place inside her house and in private. No one knew until she told a friend. On *CS*, Jim punched Liz after stopping the car on the roadside; he then threw her out onto the street. The whole neighbourhood knew. Their later confrontations also occurred on the street, in the pub or corner shop, and inside and outside their own house in the full glare of public—exterior—space.

American soaps, then, focus on the personal and the emotional; British serials look outward to the community and the means of daily existence, such as work or the lack thereof. These differences in stories are, in turn, largely rooted in differences in national ideologies: the American Dream in which anyone can achieve anything and go anywhere, versus the British John Bull ethos of strength of character and loyalty to origins. The culture of the UK also acknowledges a class structure and historical presence larger than any individual or social group. And it embodies an essential conservatism of social and geographical place not found in the ideology of the US, though perhaps existing in reality.

CS and the other British serials celebrate the cultural and social life of ordinary Britons, including the good and the bad, in the context of an identifiable and bounded community. American soaps use community, and community issues, as a backdrop for stories of emotional life and dreams of fabulous futures.

The American Dream and the Perils of Pauline

Adrienne [Johnson Kiriakis, *DOOL*, now departed] came on as a street kid who was turned into [an] incest victim ... Adrienne bore the message of the show to its viewers that any woman, no matter how ordinary her appearance and how deep her emotional scars, can marry a fabulously wealthy, handsome man. (*SOD*, October 29, 1991: 18).[79]

The non-specific fictional geography of American soaps and their production location in New York and Hollywood allow them to play with the national imagination. American soaps reflect the perception of the social homogeneity of American society and of individual social mobility in the American Dream of classlessness. In these stories, change and innovation are signs of progress.

In the dramatic tradition of melodrama, the soaps tell us that success is largely due to individual effort; that, with hard work and perhaps a lucky break, it is possible to achieve any goal; and that a successful end justifies (almost) any means. They tell us that wealth and power are preferable to a middle-class lifestyle, but they add caveats: wealth and power alone do not bring happiness, romance and love are worth more than anything, and family and integrity are the most important values. These messages are of course contradictory, but their contradictions serve dramatic and ideological purposes.

Two principal beliefs shape the American way of life. One is individualism: getting ahead of the pack. The other is patriotism: working for the common good. Successful patriots combine the two in their personal variation on the credo "What's good for General Motors is good for America." The American Dream says that by relying on personal strength and letting nothing stand in the way, anyone can succeed. America loves success stories because they reinforce personal hope for betterment and reassure the nation that, despite its glaringly unequal distribution of wealth, it is the greatest nation in the world. Linda Dano, who plays a glamorous and wealthy romance novelist on *AW*, sees it this way:

I learned early on from the audiences that they liked Felicia because she was self-made, because she didn't have anything, absolutely no money—she came from a really poor background—and she worked so hard and made it, that they never begrudged her her money or her power, which I find interesting. They relate to her. I guess it's sort of a role-model. They think, "Wow, maybe I could do that; I could achieve that." (Interview)

Al Rosenberg of *Daytime TV* explains how soaps communicate the moral lesson that social disadvantages do not have to limit potential:

Drucilla [of *Y&R*] was a street waif who fell in love with Nathan and just to show ... what she could accomplish ... she began taking ballet lessons and pulled herself up by her bootstraps and became a beautiful young lady, not only physically but spiritually and emotionally more mature also. (Interview)

Alan Filewod connects this interpretation of the American Dream with the elements of melodrama:

Drucilla in *Young and the Restless* [goes] from being a kind of homeless runaway to an aspiring model; it's because she has made the moral conversion to *pull herself up*.... You know, melodrama is ultimately *the* most moralistic of genres for that reason: it tends to reduce social issues to simple matters of individual morality. (Interview)

Note that, although social problems are discussed as social and community concerns, they are solved individually or with help from well-connected individuals. An unemployed person happens to meet a wealthy businessperson who is always able find a position in his or her company. We are to believe this in a time of major job cutbacks in the real world? Couldn't the reality of downsizing provide compelling stories?

The message dovetails with the philosophy of the conservative right: people are poor or unemployed because they do not look for work. This is not to suggest that the soaps are a mouthpiece for the right wing of political America, but that the myth of class mobility supports republican individualism, in addition to reproducing the story of Cinderella. Viewers identifying with Drucilla can experience vicariously the success story of the American Dream.

You will not find this message of social mobility in the storylines of British serials. According to Phillip Crookes, a political scientist at the University of Manchester:

A lot of American writers at the beginning of the century used to write the Andrew Carnegie sort of story: the kid picking his nails, his teeth or his nose on the sidewalk can be the corporate president and learn to run the railroad—whereas in this country the kid knows his social place and will always stay in [that] place.

[The Carnegie philosophy] is a very strong ethos: it has to do with egalitarianism; it has to do with the belief that anybody can be president; it has to do with "I'm as good as you are because *I* say so." That's North American, it's not British. (Interview)

One reason why the egalitarian ethos remains so important to America's vision of itself is precisely that it distances that nation from its colonial past, from Britain. For if the life, liberty, and pursuit of happiness for which the founders of the republic fought is largely the privilege of the already wealthy, the new democracy is no different from the old aristocracy.

But American soaps do not equate wealth and happiness. Satisfaction comes from patriotism and family. This also serves to soften the impact of the fact that, in reality, hard work and effort are not enough to guarantee success. A number of threads in the fabric of soap storylines emphasize the theme that wealth does not buy happiness. One is the primacy given to family ties and love. But the point is also driven home by powerfully negative association: many wealthy characters are extremely unhappy, and many of them obtained their money by suspect or vicious deeds. They usually remain at least partially villainous characters unless they have done something that redeems them. Even "good" rich characters' lives contain much misery. *AW*'s Felicia, for instance, may be famous and wealthy, but in the early 1990s her husband was murdered and her daughter was raped. Felicia fell right to the bottom, with the help of a lot of brandy; the only thing her money ensured was that it was very good brandy.

Most, if not all, soap villains are wealthy. Some are one-dimensional incarnations of evil, while others (like *AMC*'s Adam Chandler) combine ruthlessness in business and love with wit and sometimes true tenderness. Some get their wealth by deceit. Paulina Cory on *AW* was introduced as a scheming little imposter who had been raised in an abusive foster home on the slummy Gold Street (the same street Felicia came from). She claimed to be Mac Cory's illegitimate daughter, and, with Mac dead, there was no one to refute her claim. After she got her trust fund, Jake discovered her claim was false, and blackmailed her. However, in a memento from her deceased mother, Paulina discovered that Mac was indeed her father. She is now a thoroughly nice and good character. In an ironic twist, she and her husband, police commissioner Joe Carlino, struggled with financial problems because he refused to use her family's millions to help out.[80]

The wealth-does-not-bring-happiness theme also forges some surprising alliances between audiences and characters. New York actress Jacqueline Brookes always played soap characters who are seen at work, but often in jobs not expected to evoke great audience sympathy. During her stint as district attorney Ursula Winthrop in the soap *Secret Storm*, her character prosecuted a wealthy woman. At the same time Ms. Brookes's mother was in hospital; going to visit her one day, she got off the subway at an unstaffed exit in a rough neighbourhood:

> I heard this voice ... I realized she was screaming "Ursula, Ursula, it's Ursula!"... Out of the woodwork came about twenty of the strangest collection of people, street people, transvestites, drug addicts ... and they were so excited to meet Ursula! You would think the last person in the world they would care about would be the district attorney, but ... they loved me for getting that rich bitch. And it just really opened my eyes.... And the upshot was they said, "You're going to the hospital? We'll take you," and this whole entourage came with me through Columbia Presbyterian Hospital! Quite an extraordinary group, and loud, expansive into the hospital: "Ursula, Ursula!" (Interview)

Some who can afford, or need, to dream can look at Felicia Gallant and the other rags-to-riches characters and take hope or inspiration from them. Others may take comfort from the human miseries that are part of life, whether one is rich or poor. Still others, like Jacqueline Brookes's street-people fans, who recognize their social immobility, may champion authority figures who bring down the wealthy, even though in real life it is more likely they themselves who will be prosecuted.

Though money—the possession of, or search for, it—is central to American soaps, rarely do we glimpse the actual labour that produces it.[81] Money stands as a symbol of the American Dream and for the ideology of class mobility. Street-tough Noah on *AMC* survived by his wits, legally and illegally. For a while, his efforts to better his position were presented plausibly, within a fairytale narrative: Julia got her sister's fabulously wealthy brother-in-law, a Hungarian count, to hire him as groundskeeper. Noah did not like being a "servant" (and played the "angry young black man" well), but it was an honest job. Later, working as a hospital orderly, emptying bedpans and feeling hopeless about ever improving his lot, he was tempted to return to his previous criminal life. Julia counselled him that the prestige in doing any job is in doing it well, so he kept working. Then, a modelling agent sighted his impressive dreadlocks and body, and he experienced a meteoric rise as a model in a nation-wide jeans ad campaign. He stopped modelling, however, not seeing it as a valid or valuable career, despite the money involved. His aunt was working class, honest and proud, and his sister was a lawyer. These details seem an attempt to maintain his storyline origins while showing potential (through his sister's profession) for movement through the social classes.

Even when soaps introduce matters of money and jobs in somewhat more realistic, or at least varied, ways, they still fulfil the demands of the American Dream and of melodrama, which depends on heightened emotions and exaggerated behaviour. Melodrama works through implausibility of predicament, unexpected contact and absence, and secrets kept or revealed at critical moments. But the heroine is always rescued in the nick of time, and true love prevails.

> On the one hand [soaps] reinforce the myth of class mobility, and on the other [they tend] to work as an enforcement of class immobility, by saying, yeah, you can make it, Drucilla can make it, but is she any happier? Is this in fact a kind of ... narrative coercion, which reinforces the social structures which inhibit actual social progress? I think ultimately they would assume that they're making a very liberal social statement, but I think in fact soap operas become one of the narrative modes that really sustain and reinforce the fundamental structures of American society. (Alan Filewod, interview)

Pack Up Your Troubles:
British Realism and Nostalgia

When you've prepared spotted dick and custard for 150 under heavy artillery fire and not allowed one lump in that custard, you can do anything.

PERCY SUGDEN, CS

If American soaps are rooted in the tradition of melodrama, British serials are planted in social, or kitchen-sink, realism. *CS* and *Emmerdale* also cater to an idealized nostalgia for the past, which mourns the degeneracy of modern Britain. *CS*'s Second World War veteran Percy Sugden regularly referred disdainfully to the lack of mettle of today's "young people" compared to those who withstood the trials of wartime. He was often joined by wheelchair-bound, acerbic-tongued Maud Grimes, mother of Maureen, who, after a burglary at the cornershop she and her daughter ran, sharply told concerned neighbours, "We didn't close shop during the Blitz....We hung a sign out saying 'Business as Usual.' Not going to close for a burglary" (*CS* March 12, 1996, Canadian air date).

Percy and Maud despair over the younger generations, and celebrate the capability of Britons under siege. They are not alone. The Queen Mother earned a place in the heart of the nation, and elsewhere, by refusing to take her family out of England during the Blitz. Princess Elizabeth endeared herself to servicemen by performing her war service as a driver wearing combat clothes. Memories of such actions ensure that those women will never be included in the generalized disrespect for other royals. While Britons and tourists will pay good money to see the Crown Jewels at the Tower of London, irresponsible behaviour and lavish spending by royal hangers-on and lesser aristocracy is not accepted. And so, in a land with royalty, there is no soap about the upper classes.

Many of the characters in American soaps could be considered akin to royalty in their lifestyle and social standing. The incredible popularity of the prime-time soaps of the 1980s and 1990s—*Dallas, Dynasty, Beverly Hills 90210*, and *Melrose Place*—suggests that networks are not foisting the world of the rich on reluctant viewers. Even the relatively "ordinary," middle-class *Knots Landing*, which a British journalist described as "the nearest the Americans can bear to get to a soap about real people" (Kingsley 1989: 226, quoted in Crofts 1995: 110), became more glamorous, wealthier, and nastier in its final years.

But *Dallas* and *Dynasty* were popular in Britain for totally different reasons than in the US. Tony Warren claims that his compatriots watch these shows "with grisly fascination," to see an America that is "horrendous—grasping and greedy" (interview). One young man in a Liverpool pub agreed with those sentiments, but added that sometimes he wondered if it were possible to get that kind of wealth; if he were to emigrate, would he be able to do so well? Phillip Crookes agrees that the lure of emigration is strong for Britons because therein lies their best chance of succeeding (interview). So the dream of America, the Land of Opportunity, does have currency in the UK, despite that nation's dislike of tasteless displays of wealth. Even so, British viewers of American serials look on—whether with horror or some degree of envy, always from a distance—at a cultural narrative alien to their own.

> As a nation I think we have a suspicion of people with money. I remember Michael Caine who said, when he earned a lot of money … the difference between Britain and America was if he drove past in a huge big car in America, they said gosh, well done, I'd like to do that. And if he did it in Britain, they'd probably scrape a coin down the side of the car! I disagree … but I think he made a point: that the British generally do not like people flaunting their money. And the grave danger of playing upper-classdom [on TV] is that you show lots of money, big houses, lots of spending … and therefore you tend not

to have sympathy for the character.... I don't think an awful lot of people have sympathy with upper-class people when they've got problems, because they've got lots of money and most of it is inherited. They've not earned it ... when they've got problems you're likely to say, well I'm glad they got something wrong with them. (Reynolds, interview)

Britons, according to Reynolds, do not object to wealth acquired through work (though flaunting wealth is generally seen as *déclassé*), but wealth does not provide entry to the upper classes. American audiences approve of wealth acquired by one's efforts—indeed, hard-earned wealth is fundamental to the Andew Carnegie myth—and therefore most American soap millionaires are self-made, illustrating the American Dream. *Y&R's* Victor Newman grew up in an orphanage, and John Abbot built Jabot Cosmetics from the ground up; *AMC's* Adam Chandler and Palmer Cortlandt both grew up in Pigeon Hollow, West Virginia, hardly a playground for the rich. On British serials, by contrast, even those who work for their fortunes are not presented in a good light: *CS's* Mike Baldwin is a borderline "scoff-law" and schemer, *Emmerdale's* resident rich man gained his money by building holiday tourist homes, thereby diluting community solidarity by encouraging outsiders. Britons and Americans react very differently to the Horatio Alger scenario: American viewers dream of following in Alger's footsteps, Britons assume he'll never get anywhere. Because they don't believe the "Dream," they do not want to see its portrayal on television, at least not on their own programs.

The social message celebrated in British serials is the strength of the ordinary working man and woman, the backbone of the nation. We see this even in *Brookside's* middle-class struggles to deal with urban violence and crime or the demands children make of financially hard-pressed parents for the current "in" brand of sneakers; in *EE's* struggle to deal with London poverty, homelessness, and crime; in *Emmerdale's* efforts to maintain a viable rural farming heritage in the face of collapsing agricultural economics and "invasion" by tourists and transplanted southerners; and in *CS's* wartime nostalgia. In all, people struggle to stay afloat and sometimes fail, but in the end loyalty to their own group keeps them going.

This theme of group solidarity in the face of all odds has been seen before: in Britain's John Bull ideology, which celebrates the establishment and administration of a great empire, as well as the efforts of the "common man" to provide the wealth with which to do it, and in Second World War propaganda efforts, which recognized the critical contributions of working men and women. During that conflict Britons were called upon to scrimp, save, and give their time, even their pots and pans, to the war effort. It was a frightening time, but also an exhilarating one. Surviving the bombs and coping with scarcities demanded strength of will and resourcefulness. Rising to these challenges and enjoying occasional luxuries gave pleasure—of the moment and in later reflection—and provided a standard by which later generations could be tried and found wanting: "What *she'd* have been like in the Blitz I can't think," said Maude about her daughter's reaction to the burglary of their shop (*CS*, March 13, 1996).

Maude and Percy kept alive memories of the Second World War fifty years after its end, but the theme of strength under fire has always under-lined the storylines:

> It's almost like they say that you see the best about British people when they're on the down—like during the war, you saw the best of everybody ... they all had a problem together, therefore they all rallied round and sang songs and, you know, tried to make themselves cheer up.... And I think that's what they almost want to see with *Coronation Street*, they want to see people who are down, who are laughing despite their problems. (Reynolds, interview)

Or, in the words of Ena Sharples, "When there's a war, we get a lot of nice souls. Everybody's nice to everybody else. Nobody bothers about dressing up. It's funny what war does to folk." The 1964 episode of *CS* in which Ena reminisces about the war is interesting in its development of this theme, especially in light of what was happening in England at the time. The Beatles had taken over the UK and the world, and the Merseybeat was flooding pop music stations. Mods and rockers were battling out their ideological principles in clothing choice in the streets; Carnaby Street and other London market areas were setting international fashion standards for the young. As Tony Warren said, "The sixties started here, down the road in Liverpool.... 'Swinging London' was not just a journalistic invention" (interview). In the midst of this explosion of youth culture, in 1964, *CS* aired an episode in which Stan Ogden dug up an undetonated Second World War bomb in Albert Tatlock's back garden. Military experts were called in, and residents were evacuated to the basement of the Glad Tidings Hall. Ena Sharples, hall caretaker and Second World War air raid patrol (ARP) warden, took command. She found her warden's helmet and donned it, establishing her control over the situation. When Mr. Tatlock contested her authority, she set him straight as to her higher rank. The fastidious Annie Walker reluctantly came to the hall, after imploring her husband, "Do we really have to mingle?" All settled in around the table, Minnie Caldwell's eyes shone with excitement, and talk began about the fun of surviving real air raids. The young people initially were bored, but eventually the whole group began to sing, starting with "White Cliffs of Dover," then "Over There," then "We'll Meet Again."

Outside, two soldiers dismantled the bomb and talked about their childhood memories of the war. One was from Manchester, one from London, so there was an element of rivalry over which city got the worst from "Jerry," and which city's people stood up the best. After the bomb was defused, the senior officer said, "I suppose we'd better give them the allclear. They're probably scared to death down that shelter." The young policeman who came to tell them it was safe was amazed to see all, young and old, dancing and singing "Mares eat oats and does eat oats ..." And, in keeping with the wartime tradition, after the all-clear was sounded Ena began singing "Keep the Homes Fires Burning," and all joined in.

For *CS* in particular, then, war is one acid test of a people's mettle. A second theme by which the strength of the British people is conveyed, in all the serials, is the solidarity of community. This, once again, reflects the importance of social class, and of sticking to one's own, in British society.

Admittedly, the details of "one's station" or "one's own" have altered over time. The rigours of working-class life have lessened or changed on the Street since its early days. One commentator sees this as evidence for *CS*'s intrinsic sentimentalization of "a vanishing world":

> Early programmes were much [quicker] to use as part of their realism the washing drying round the fire.... Now the occasional shots of fish and chips in newspaper on the table at the Ogdens are used to show the Ogdens as outsiders who let the side down by such sleaziness. (Jordan 1981: 35)

Harry Elton provides a counterpoint: "In the original street, people were taking baths in zinc tubs on a Saturday night, and they were going to outhouses out in the backyard because they didn't have indoor sanitation" (interview). That has changed; it would indeed be nostalgic sentimentalism if it had not. And social relations and attitudes have changed as well. But much of the over-arching thematic structure persists; soap characters still manifest a strong Us-versus-Them mentality and are wont to close ranks against Them. Mike Baldwin, despite over twenty years of residence on the Street, is still a "Londoner," still not trusted, and with his aspirations to wealth remains an outsider even to his friends. Too much ambition is seen as suspicious and likely to come to no good. When the Duckworths inherited a sizable sum in Jack's brother's will, the Street residents expected their downfall, especially in light of Vera's gloating and putting on airs. When they bought the Rovers Return and promptly encountered difficulties in running it, residents (and viewers) waited with bated breath to see just how fast they would lose everything. They weren't disappointed. Financial problems soon beset Jack and Vera.

At the root of this animosity towards getting above one's place is the fact that social station has long been clearly defined in Britain. The boundaries have become less inflexible, but they still exist. Former prime minister Margaret Thatcher may have spoken with pride of being a grocer's daughter, but she took elocution lessons to rid herself of her working-class accent. Compare this to the US, where millionaire Ross Perot used his Texan accent to garner support from "ordinary" people in a presidential election campaign. The historical presence of a rich aristocracy in Britain is a constant reminder of class privilege, even if the aristocrats must nowadays turn their estates into tourist sites to maintain them.

While class barriers may not be as rigid, and correlation of class and money not fit as neatly as in the past, the perception of social class still informs British ideology, and that fact is reflected in television serials. To compare the British and American national ideologies, put them in geographical terms. Visualize the English countryside: clearly and neatly laid-out fields, bounded by stone fences or hedgerows, impenetrable and unchanging. Now visualize the American (or Canadian) prairies: vast fields unending as far as the eye can see, bordered by rail or barbed wire fences that are easy to slip through.

Harry Elton, who is Canadian but lived in the UK throughout the 1950s, has pondered the British class structure and the way in which cultural mythologies influence expression of the "self":

> I think for those of us who are raised in North America it is almost impossible to really understand how that class system worked, and how iron-clad were the barriers.... I actually had spent a lot of my youth in Detroit, in the "melting pot," and the American myth was what I grew up with. There was nothing—it didn't matter where I came from, what my [parents] did, I could be president if I bloody well wanted to be president.
>
> It was even seductive for Canadians when we went [to the UK]. After the war the British had a [very particular] feeling about Canadians.... They had a love/hate thing for the Americans, and they admired a lot of things the Americans did but they disliked a lot of the others. So they seized on the Canadians as the perfect examples of North Americans. They liked to believe that we had all the good things and none of the bad things. And that meant that we could go anywhere and do anything.
>
> We had a social mobility that was very deceptive. It took a long time to realize that although I could go anywhere and it didn't mat-

ter whether I knew which fork to pick up or how I talked, my British colleagues, if they were born into the working class, couldn't go everywhere.

...The people stuck together, they were in it together! They were members of a class, they didn't aspire to become leaders of the nation or captains of industry. Now obviously, there were exceptions to that, and obviously that society isn't nearly as hidebound now as it used to be. But I think that, in a sense, the soaps—or serial storytelling—do reflect the myths of the nation in which they occur. (Interview)

Conclusion

In different ways, British and American serials have dealt with the presentation of a social view based on their formulas of storytelling components. They have also tried to be socially responsible and dramatically relevant by addressing social concerns of the day. Often, they do little more than "circulate social issues," as Alan Filewod says. He is right in saying that soaps raise issues, but rarely get at the roots. Nonetheless, they may serve a purpose in slowly introducing, to the narrow or cloistered, worlds other than their own. At their best, that is what American and British soaps do; at their worst, they trivialize or distort important social matters.

Six:
Conclusion:
Who Watches, Why, and What Soaps Tell Us About Ourselves

The American soaps are total, complete escapism....You just want to sit and look at Iris Carrington in full flowing silk nighties with wonderful dressing gowns over them, drinking martinis, and go: of course that's how I'm supposed to live, this is the American Dream.

COLLEEN O'TOOLE, CANADIAN SOAP FAN

Such silly stories ... they don't do things like that in England, do they. It's a bit weird, really.

TWO WOMEN FROM MANSFIELD, NOTTINGHAMSHIRE,
TALKING ABOUT AMERICAN SOAPS

NO ONE gets hooked on a soap on first viewing. To the uninitiated, they make little sense: a scene that obviously is a continuation of a conversation cuts away to totally different people discussing a totally different issue, and at the end of the episode the loose ends are still untied. On traditional sit-coms or dramatic series, the first-time viewer typically sees a situation posed, with misunderstandings and attempts to understand, culminating in resolution (the classic Aristotelian formula). A viewer either likes the story and actors and tunes in next week—or does not. But on soaps, stories may be months or years in the unfolding. This is one reason why soaps are less immediately palatable; like caviar, soap-watching is an acquired taste. And like other acquired tastes, appreciation usually follows on exposure in the right circumstances, with time to learn and understand. That is why many people start watching soaps when they are ill, unemployed, or somehow find themselves at home with nothing to do:

People often hit *Coronation Street* at a low ... ebb in their lives, and it's there and it's almost like a friend, and if it sees them through the bad times, they'll probably go away from it after the bad times. ... But then later, maybe they'll not hit the bad times again, but when they come up against [*CS*] the next time, they remember it as something warm, something friendly and something familiar, and they return to it. (Warren, interview)

Once you comprehend the storylines, you get to know the characters who people them. You acquire likes and dislikes, identify those characters who bore or annoy you or remind you of yourself. Attachment is often uniquely intense, as attested by the lyrics of a popular Newfoundland song of the early 1980s, sung by Rex Hemeon:

Bingo and *Another World,* that's all I ever hear.
It's getting so I can't sit home and enjoy a bottle of beer.
Between Rachel and the jackpot, I'm slowly going mad.
I've seen people before possessed, but girl you got it bad.

One of my students reports that his grandparents daily announce, "The program is coming on ...," the firm signal to leave or shut up and watch TV. His grandparents watch more than one television show, but their soap is *the* program, and its airtime is sacrosanct. Two other students told me, "Mother just said, 'my stories are starting.'" Husband and children knew this was their cue to disappear, giving mother her only guaranteed quiet time of the day. Is time for the stories important to such women only for the pleasures of viewing, or as a device that eases intra-family negotiation of personal time and space? After all, mothers not employed outside the home are on-call twenty-four hours a day, and "Don't bug me, I want to stare out the window" generally does not go over well with children and husbands wanting a question answered or a button sewn on. The regular daily schedule of soap operas and their unending, serial nature allow them to be established as a firm demarcation of time that is, inviolably, mother's, and this time for herself can be negotiated without hurt feelings and family turmoil.

Within this protected zone of time, soap-viewing can serve further needs:

The hour of one's favorite soap is a time for being alone with one's animated, talking picture book. It is also a form of "cuddle literature" for grown-ups ... it takes place, like a bedtime story, according to a fixed routine and within a trusted setting. (Porter 1977: 782)

The simple familiarity, the *ritual*, of viewing can soothe overburdened nerves. As well, soaps allow adults coping with the pressures of work, family, and money a time-out to watch other people's problems. Soaps, like bedtime stories, raise perils that are removed from the viewer, and there will be a happy ending at some point, for a little while. And when you're caught up in and worried about the situations the characters find themselves in, that is time during which "you're not worrying about what your kids are doing. You can [worry over the characters] ... and then you can leave it behind" (Filewod, interview). Porter agrees:

> Watching soap opera involves a combination of sympathy and distance, of observing unobserved under conditions that titillate but finally leave you untouched. Like Gulliver among the Lilliputians, one can look patronizingly down from among cushions into a miniaturized world of two-dimensional dolls. (Porter 1977: 782–83)[82]

For those whose primary need is not for a bit of seclusion or time of their own, watching with others enhances the enjoyment of viewing by adding the pleasure of talking about events on-screen. Of course, a good chat is possible even if viewing is not shared.[83] If he misses an episode, says Filewod, "I'll ask my wife, so what happened yesterday? I didn't see [*Y&R*]. And she'll fill me in, and then it's a great gossip session" (interview).

The Changing Family of Fans

It used to be that many fans grew up with their soaps. At public events featuring soap actors, says actor Jay Hammer, it is not uncommon to see three generations of fans, male and female (interview). An *ATWT* long-time viewer told me she started watching at age eleven with her grandmother, who enlisted first her daughter and then her granddaughter as companion viewers. Generalized over thousands of viewers, this phenomenon, according to Lilana Novakovich, accounts for *AW*'s greater popularity in Canada than in the US: it was the first on a Canadian network. As a result, "It's got a history ... [people will say] it was my mother's story, my aunt's story, and so it's become my story" (interview). Soaps are shared family "property."

They are also community property. Before cable and satellites, many hinterland communities received only one channel. In the northern BC Tsimshian village where I watched my first soap, *AW* was the only one available, so everyone knew it, and conversation easily switched between events of the village and events in Bay City. This can be very confusing. A former teacher in coastal Labrador who did not watch "the story" told me of her panic when a student raced into class saying, "so-and-so has died!"

Students eventually got her to understand that it was a favourite soap character, not a community resident. She started watching, or at least ensured she was kept up-to-date.

In such circumstances, a community makes viewing a particular soap part of its daily routine and discourse, part of how its members connect and converse with each other. Even if another soap became available, community members would not be able to switch allegiance entirely to it without paying some price in community participation.

Allegiances to soaps can of course become dispersed, but this occurs gradually, slowly spreading over the breadth of a community. With an increase in channels, family or community attachment to a single soap is lessened. In Newfoundland, with only two channels (without cable) it is possible to watch soaps from 12:30 to 5:30 every weekday afternoon (with only one half-hour exception). With cable, the choice doubles, and so communities and families may not share the same story. In my neighbour's family, for instance, the mother watches *Y&R*, the daughter watches *Y&R* and *CS*, and the son watches *OLTL*.

Even when all family or community members don't watch the same soap, they remain community property. Their stories and structure have enough similarity that the main issues of plotlines can be discussed, even if the minute points of plot and character are not familiar to all discussants. And due to the pervasiveness of television and to conversations with family and friends, most families and neighbours to some extent are able to discuss all of the soaps. I know I can enter any house in my community, even that of perfect strangers, and mention Nikki and Victor, Erica and Dimitri, Lucky and Liz—someone, if not everyone, will know who I'm talking about. And if they mention Eric and Stephanie or Sheila, I will know something about these characters. Soap families are shared by millions.

Technology, in addition to greatly expanding our viewing options, has altered *how* we watch. Prior to VCRs and cable, you watched when a show aired in your area. If you had no access to a television at that time, you could not watch. Now, cable allows viewers to tune in to stations in different time zones. VCRs allow even greater flexibility: viewers can tape the shows and watch at their convenience.[84] But access to both cable stations in different time zones and to VCRs can alter patterns of soap gossip. In Newfoundland, for example, *Y&R* airs in early evening from Alberta. If you watch it from 12:30 to 1:30 p.m. on Newfoundland TV, you can't ask your neighbour his or her opinion of what Nikki did if that neighbour watches the Alberta broadcast, or watches at 2 a.m. on videotape.

Videotaping in particular allows fans to tailor their viewing circumstances, and develop much more personalized rituals. And people do have their little rituals. A Toronto businesswoman told me her routine after the week's work is finished is to take a big bowl of popcorn to bed on Saturday night, turn on the VCR, and watch a week's worth of episodes of her story. A friend's retired parents tape the full week's episodes of *GH* even though they are generally home during its broadcast time. Instead they settle in for a long, cozy Sunday morning watching them. Even when away, they prefer to get someone to tape the week's show for them and to watch when they get home—they do not want to disturb the show's sequence or their ritual. *CS*, with its end-of-week omnibus repeat airing, is particularly well suited for ritual, social viewing even without a VCR. Many fans told me it is Sunday routine to get together with friends to watch, and then discuss the episodes' and their own week's events.[85]

New technology, as well as providing new ways of watching the soaps, has also provided new methods for chatting about them. If you cannot discuss Nikki's actions with friends, with a computer and an e-mail account you can do so with the world. The internet has dramatically affected how fans gather information on the stories and actors as well as how they can discuss stories with others. Various types of user groups for individual soaps can be subscribed to, and home pages for each soap exist on the worldwide web, performing some of the functions of soap magazines. These magazines have also gone on-line, with home pages and internet discussion groups. Many home pages and on-line chats are organized by the soap industry. But fans themselves have not been idle: home pages and "chat rooms" as well as the e-mail news group category "*rats*" (an acronym for rec.arts.tv.soaps) are organized by fans.[86] Within *rats* there is one list for *ABC* soaps, another for *CBS*, and "misc.," which includes *NBC*. There are news groups and many websites for British serials, providing "official" and unofficial histories and information on the shows. Internet communication venues are very popular with fans. For example, the *rats* user groups may each have well over a thousand messages each month. Some "Ratsafarians," as participants call themselves, put considerable effort into their on-line communications:

> Daily updates analyzing each episode are written and posted by Ratsafarian volunteers, each responsible for a specific day.... After enthusiastic AMC viewers began posting messages "in character" as their FAC (Favorite AMC Character), the idea spread throughout RATS as F★C's (the ★ stands for the first letter of the show). Since popular characters went fast, some FAC's decided to "incorporate," offering shares ... to other readers ... The first FGC Kevin (GH) acts as CEO of "Kevin Unlimited."... Shawne Adelman jumped at the chance to become "keeper of the prom picture" (FGC Stone, deceased, GH) because Stone was "my favorite character and someone has to keep an eye on that very important picture." (*SOD*, April 9, 1996: 57-58)

What do fans get from these groups? They say that they get the same thing they have always got from talking with each other: "They know who Erica is and why she can drive you crazy. The people on RATS understand why soaps are important to me, and that's such a relief"; and "Coming to RATS every day is like coming home" (*SOD*, April 9, 1996: 58). In a word: *community.*

The internet has added to the ease with which soap fans can communicate within that community. It casts a wider net, allowing communication with the whole world; but it also casts a shallower, more depersonalized one. The range of dialogue is greatly narrowed: we know nothing about the people with whom we are talking except what they say about the soaps, nor are we likely to. Both on-line or in person, fans discuss all aspects of soaps, in both serious and humorous ways. But e-mail discussion is unlikely to spill over into real life. On-line correspondents will discuss, say, the circumstances of a soap divorce, but they are unlikely to talk about their own. There are exceptions: one storyline in which Holly and Fletcher of *GL* had a Down's Syndrome baby was discussed, and appreciated, by on-line parents of Down's Syndrome children. In general, however, face-to-face chats about soap stories are more likely than electronic ones to evoke disclosure of personal details.

On-line soap fans may have nothing in common with each other, aside from their interest in a particular show and access to communications software.[87] Through extended "lurking" (on-line reading but not posting messages), I have learned that participants fall within the full demographic spectrum, from teens to grandparents, students to secretaries and lawyers, married and single, gay and straight. Arguments can erupt over social issues presented in the stories, or over an offhand comment, and the full array of politicized points of views are expressed, politely and not so politely.

Because cyberspace fandom reflects the demographic spread of soap fans around the world, it is a fertile source for analysts, who have long sought to ascertain if there are patterns in who watches the soaps and how they watch. But researchers have been investigating those questions since well before the advent of the internet, resulting in an extensive literature on soap fans and soap watching. Quite a few of these studies, especially empirical ones, involve university students,[88] presumably because they are a captive audience for professors, but also because students often watch as a group in campus lounges, and so the study can also address the group dynamics of viewing. Studies of non-student adult audiences, on the other hand, reveal more variety in the types of "gossip" about the soaps. Because the available analyses are extensive, and because the reader, if interested, can easily read these studies first hand, I will not reiterate them here; instead I will try to convey some impression of how soaps mesh with daily life by presenting two studies of different ways in which women use them to form shared subcultures.

The first study, by Dorothy Hobson, focuses on the female employees of a British telephone sales office and their discussions, both serious and silly, of what they liked and disliked in the various serials. On the serious side, these women discussed how the stories related to their own lives, for instance by comparing their real-life partners with the characters on a soap:

> "If my Alan was as vile as Pete, I think I'd go off with Willmott-Brown!"
>
> The comments ... are offered only in a joking manner ... One particular woman revealed not only her interest in soap operas but also ... "her own particular domestic hell" ... although she never prophesied as to what she would do if she were in the position of someone in a television drama, it did provide a means for her to talk about the way that she experienced her own life. (Hobson 1990: 64-5)

Women who were not living in situations similar to those in storylines discussed what they would do if they were; those whose lives did parallel the situations of the serials would frequently try to probe further into those opinions:

> As in, "But what if you loved him? But what if he said ...?" ... They would try to get the reactions from the other girls. I suppose it was a way to assess their own feelings and situations.
>
> The use of events within fiction to explore experiences that were perhaps too personal or painful to talk about ... is a beneficial and creative way of extending the value of the program into their own lives. (Hobson 1990: 65)

Lessons for life can be gleaned directly from the soaps, but, especially when painful, they can be revealed and discussed more usefully with others. An indication of the value for women, and the possible threat to the status quo, of this kind of chat is seen in Hobson's example of "Vicky." Her domineering husband would not let her watch the soaps if he was home, though she loved them (Hobson 1990: 64). Her female co-workers provided a means for her to catch up on the stories and, more importantly, to obtain comfort and indirect advice on her domestic situation. Presumably, her husband, if he knew, would take a dim view of both.

Another researcher discusses how *CS* validates women's interests:

> Soap opera may be the opium of the masses of women, but like religion, it may also be ... a context in which women can ambiguously

express *both* good-humoured acceptance of their oppression *and* recognition of that oppression, and some equally good-humoured protest against it. In the words of Sheila Rowbotham, it is an expression and celebration of the way in which:

> women have resolutely manoeuvred for a better position ... by shifting for themselves, turning the tables, ruling the roost, wearing the trousers, hen-pecking, gossiping, hustling or ... just "going drip drip at him" (Rowbotham 1979).

No wonder men dislike it! (Lovell 1981: 51)

Among the women in the office Hobson discusses, the soaps do not just spark discussion about interpersonal matters on the soaps or in their own lives. They also provide jumping-off points for considering wider social and political issues. And the myth that people who watch television are not using their time to the full is demolished by the range of views these women expressed and explored through their use of television:

> "We have touched on every single subject from AIDS,... homosexuals, and some people would say, 'I think that it is disgusting', and somebody else said, 'Do you mind, my brother's gay' ... then you would talk about it. We have talked about ... racism, people's experience, why certain people are prejudiced. Some people would freely admit they were prejudiced and try to justify [it].... And that was OK because they were trying to go one step towards not being prejudiced". (Hobson 1990: 70)

While the women ensured that they met their sales quotas each day, they did not let customers get in the way of important talk:

> "If you were ... just about to put the world right on what you thought about Nicaragua and somebody says, 'Jacqui, I've got Neil from Blackwoods on the telephone' ... he was probably ringing to complain about something anyway, so you would wait until you had finished the conversation and then ring him back to sort out his problem." (1990:71)

The women of Hobson's study clearly created an environment contoured to their needs and interests within their workplace. As Hobson says, they "were skilled in bringing their culture into their workplace.... It is the interweaving of the narratives of fictions with the narratives of their reality that formed the basis for ... creating their own culture within their workplace" (1990: 71).

Another feminist analyst, Mary Ellen Brown, discusses the role of "gossip" as a feminine, and potentially subversive, form of discourse. Among other aspects of soaps British fans liked, some commented on their humour, particularly as a tool of empowerment wielded by women. Of *EE* one group said:

> *E*:   The language ... the humour is Cockney and it's very
>   sharp.... That's definitely some of the pleasure in watching
>   it. It's the way things are said.... The put-downs, the rude-
>   ness, all very stylised really.
>
> *ME*:   Well, the power of the women seems to have to do with
>   their ... [sic]
>
> *E*:   Their mouths. (Laughs.) (Brown 1990: 193)

Brown also discusses how women quote or mimic soap characters, and how that adds to the pleasure of watching and talking about them, and, perhaps more relevantly, how mimicry is another empowering device. About *CS* they say:

> *E*:   "You'd be talking about things in general and you'd sud-
>   denly throw in a line from Mavis.... You'd say something in
>   a Mavis voice. I mean there's great lines from Bet Lynch
>   that you ... things like put-downs mainly, mainly probably
>   put-downs to men which is why she is popular in her role
>   as a barmaid ...
>   He'd [wannabe ladies' man Fred Gee] be preening him-
>   self in front of the mirror ... and he'd say, 'How do I look
>   then, Lynch?' and she'd say, 'Oh, you look like a well-
>   scrubbed pig.' So you'd use that line." (Brown 1990: 193)

As Brown points out, such borrowings serve a dual purpose: they become "a performance on the part of the soaps fan, acting out in the spirit of play and in the course of other conversation"; but as well, "the ability to pick up on the performance also defines a fan's membership in a group ... who recognise and speak the language" (1990: 193-94). Quoting, in other words, can be used to distinguish "insiders" and "outsiders." Brown sees a similar kind of "secret society" code employed by a young Australian fan of *DOOL*, who

carries a photograph of Bo and Hope ... and shows the picture to her friends as if the picture were of real relatives or friends—a mini-performance based on a fantasy connection with these characters. This is also an act of resistance when played against parental disapproval of soaps. (1990: 194)

It is also a signal: other fans of *DOOL* will recognize the photograph, which will allow her fantasy or joke to be shared. Again, we encounter the bonds of community, a source of pleasure.

The convoluted histories and genealogies of soaps also provide insider status for those who can remember and keep straight all the permutations and convolutions of plot. Soap history flies in the face of "official history" understood as "orderly and unified cause-and-effect relationships," as do soap genealogies, which are rarely straightforward, Brown argues, quoting Foucault's description of real genealogies as having an "inherently uncontrollable disorder" (1990: 196). And long-term soap viewers are the keepers of the family history. They are the equivalent of the "griots" of African traditional societies, the keepers of tribal history who pass it on to successive generations through oral storytelling. Their task is no easy one, given the soaps' long-lived fictional histories and complicated relationships. Consider one group discussion of *DOOL*:

> S: Oh, Alex and Marie. They weren't married. Marie was a nun. Before [that] she lived in New York. Even before that there was Tom Horton, Jr., who had amnesia and ... he wandered back to Salem with plastic surgery and nobody knew him ...
>
> He fell in love with his sister, Marie. And they ... were going to get married and all of sudden [he] remembered. So Marie ... fled ... then later on she went into a convent.... But meanwhile, when nobody knew where she was, she went to New York and had an affair with Alex and had a baby.
>
> ME: So he and Marie had a daughter?
>
> S: I'd forgotten about her. She [the daughter] got married.... Who did she get married to?
>
> K: She married Joshua. She was engaged to Jake, the Salem Strangler. (Brown 1990: 197)

There is much demand for this kind of "historical" information; soap magazine letters columns are filled with queries such as this one:

> I work with several ladies in an office, and we are all big viewers of
> *Young and Restless*. We want to know: What was the name of Brad's
> first wife (before Traci) and what happened to her? Didn't she put
> Brad in a cage? (*SOD*, May 7, 1996: 137)

If these fans had had a soap "griot" in their office, they would have had their
answer. Yet despite the demand for such information, these living reposito-
ries of soap lore are not greatly appreciated by those at the helm of the
industry, who prefer to cater to other demographic groups. Mimi Torchin of
Soap Opera Weekly once wrote an editorial about the way soaps target the
prime advertising market of 18- to 49-year-olds. She received an over-
whelming response along the lines of the following:

> I would be considered three years beyond the "cutting edge," yet I
> have invested 14 long years as a loyal fan to the No. 1 soap ... my
> home has become a meeting place to see the show....Without my fos-
> sil wisdom many of these 20- to 49-year-old viewers in our group of
> 17 loyal watchers would never have gotten interested! However, with
> the storylines presented to us ... younger characters and simple plots,
> we are ceasing to love a show from which we get no respect. (*SOW*,
> April 16, 1996: 41)

Other letters to Ms. Torchin made pointed reference to the purchasing
power of those in the older, neglected group. But even aside from financial
considerations, soaps' producers might do well to remember the amount of
time older fans have invested in characters and stories as well as their role in
recruiting the next generation of viewers.

Ignoring the desires of long-faithful viewers is one source of audience
alienation; there are of course many others. Two that are common across all
viewer categories are stories that drag on for too long and become boring,
and stories that take bizarre turns. In response, fans either stop watching or,
ironically, they continue despite the waning appeal of the story itself, mor-
bidly fascinated to see just for how long or how far over the top the story
is going to go. One example of a storyline that exerted this mixed pull on
viewers was the satanic possession of Marlena on *DOOL* discussed earlier.

E-mail lines certainly indicated frustration and boredom with the continued byzantine, dragged-out plots *DOOL* ran in the first half of 1996.
One example from May 10:

> H: I started watching DOOL about 13 years ago (when Kayla
>   was on) and I tuned in every day. I tuned out after the
>   New Year's Eve murder and have just returned a year ago. I

was all caught up in about 10 minutes! I only watch now
on Fridays as this is all I need to see to keep me informed!
Don't any of these people work? Are they all just very rich?
If so I want to move to Salem! And what about their kids?
No one is ever watching them! I haven't seen Sean D. in
about a month! And before that he was in Arimid for like 3
weeks, what about school?

I agree that some of the soaps' writers and producers have allowed a certain
predictability and lethargic pacing to mar the storylines. In response, I
amused myself by thinking about doing a one-page dialogue summary of all
the main story lines for those months. Since each set of characters is
involved in only one endeavour or thought-pattern, and says the same thing
over and over, it is possible.

Jack to Peter and/or Jennifer, "I'm going to prove you/he are/is a
murderer and crook"; Jennifer to Jack and/or Peter, "I believe in
Peter/you. He/you is/are a good man." Sami, Vivian, Kristen, Lucas,
Stephano: "I'll make him/her learn to love me."

The list can go on; but the point is that such predictability can only dampen
audience enjoyment.

At this point, judging by the opinions expressed on e-mail groups, some
viewers react by flipping through channels, shopping for a new soap. Others
just turn off the TV and read a book during their usual storytime. Still others dig in their heels and hope for a return to good writing. And some take
a sort of ghoulish pleasure in seeing just how inane plots can get.

The appeal of the saga

Soap fans watch to follow the tribulations and loves of fictional characters
in much the same way people read thick, multigenerational family saga novels. But when you read a novel you "see" the characters only in your head,
whereas soaps are brought to you through the efforts of real-life actors,
writers, and producers, all of whom leave their indelible stamp, and all of
whom may leave and be replaced. All of this potential for change must be
kept in mind by viewers, which places certain constraints on the way in
which soaps are viewed: viewers cannot just submerge themselves in an
imaginary world, for today's heroine may have a totally different face and
aspect tomorrow. Soap opera viewing, in other words, operates on several
levels. The complexity of viewing of American soaps can be traced in Louise
Spence's explanation of the title of her article "They killed off Marlena, but
...":

The title of this essay comes from a conversation between ... my
mother and grandmother.... My grandmother hadn't seen [*DOOL*] in
some time:

> *Mother:*   "They killed off Marlena, but she is on another show now."
>
> *Grandmother:*   "Who did it?"
>
> *Mother:*   "The same guy who's been trying to for a while." (1995:
>   182)

Here we see a switch from "they" (the real-life people who produce the
show) to the fictional character of Marlena; then to the real actress who
played Marlena, who is appearing in another show; and finally back to the
fictional characters, and specifically which of them killed her. In this
exchange, Spence sees a perfectly understood and effortless switch from
reality to story, something she says is not understood by those who do not
watch soaps. The popular image of soap fans is "someone who can't tell the
difference between reality and fiction" (Spence 1995: 182). But except for a
delusional minority who are unable to grasp this difference, fans switch
conversational gears between the two so smoothly as to escape the notice of
the uninitiated eavesdropper. This kind of switching is not uncommon in
discussion of any entertainment programming, but is more noticeable in
North American soap opera chat because soaps and soap watching form a
media subculture. If one does not watch soap operas, it is hard to have the
general level of information that is hard to avoid with popular prime-time
series. The "who shot JR?" mania that swept the world in 1980 after the sea-
son-ending cliffhanger on *Dallas* is the best example: you'd have to be living in a cave not to have known about that event. The mainstream
entertainment press hype around *Friends, Seinfeld,* and *Melrose Place* provide
more recent examples.

Fans' use of humour in discussions of the soaps provides further evidence
of the subtlety they bring to their viewing. For, at the same time as they
become caught up in the drama of the stories, viewers can also find the
coilings and absurdities of plot funny. For instance, during the group discussion of *DOOL* mentioned above, tracing the doings of Alex and Marie, the
revelation that Marie's daughter had married Jake, the "Salem Strangler,"
occasioned much hilarity:

> The humour takes in not only the absurdity of the specific situation
> but also the character's history ... she has been subjected to the most
> absurdly terrible (and, because of the excess, humorous) series of
> tragedies that one can imagine.... The same viewers who, at the

moment of viewing, enter wholeheartedly into the pathos of a particular situation, at the level of metadiscourse are quite capable of laughing at the same event. (Brown 1990: 197-98)

It is, as Brown suggests, the cumulative effect of such tragedies and twists and turns that provides the humour even as, in the moment, the individual events may be moving. Both enthralled and coolly observant, the viewer is simultaneously watching on two distinct levels.

Soap chat, in general, switches between multiple levels and topics: story content; opinion and analysis of storyline; the real lives of actors, producers, and writers; and how issues relate to viewers' realities and societal concerns. The story itself may become a conduit for talk about other matters, as Hobson discussed, or simply provide ways to gossip about the goings-on in other peoples' lives. If that gossip is malignant, as one *rats* participant told *SOD*, well, no-one is harmed.[89] Soaps also provide fodder for easy chat between strangers or friends. Especially in these last "pleasures" of soaps as sources of conversation, the particular content of the story may be less important than the sharing of opinions, the interpersonal contact, it makes possible:

> I realise that the real function of soap opera is to provide gossip. The people I know ... get more pleasure out of talking about them and filling each other in than they do actually watching the program. Watching the program is tracking the information: Okay, here's what Sheila and Lauren are doing; oh, this is really stupid, I'm going to go get a coffee. But later on, it's: Did you see what happened? That jerk! Did you miss it? Well, let me tell you what happened yesterday. (Filewod, interview)

And lest we forget, gossip in this sense is a far from trivial device. Soaps function as social lubricants; they are highly effective means of bridging interpersonal distances. They can, in fact, make friends of strangers, as I have seen in my own life. When working on a script about soaps for radio, I became friends with a CBC newsreader because we both watch *DOOL*. She readily admitted to watching *CS*: "It's real life, not like the American ones." When I said I liked American ones too, she admitted her secret vice: *DOOL*. Tellingly, we never discussed American soaps when others were in the room; we didn't want to call down on our heads the stereotype of soap fans as women with shallow minds and narrow lives. And shortly after the Valentine's Day *SOD* Awards one year, a grocery store cashier noted the soap magazine I had included among my purchases and cheerfully ignored the line-up behind me as she told me who had won what at the awards ceremonies.

The bond between devotees of soaps can even be strong enough to span cultures. In one episode of the sitcom *The Nanny*, the main character, Miss Fine, was arrested for inadvertently stealing an infant. In confrontation with the distraught non-English-speaking mother, Miss Fine mentioned a similar situation involving Nikki on *Y&R* years before. Instant friendship and eager attempts at communication ensued.[90]

One viewer, Kelli Beveridge of St. Catherine's, Ontario, so aptly summarized for me via e-mail the ways and reasons viewers adopt a soap—how one comes to a particular soap (the now cancelled *The City*, formerly *Loving*), reasons for watching, limits of fidelity to a story, sharing it with others, and attention to the ways stories mesh with reality—that I give her the last word.[91]

I was watching *DOOL* but got turned off by the devil storyline, my sister was watching *Loving* (and she always taped it ... and played it back, "Watch this, Kelli") so I started watching the little clips she pulled out for me (mostly about Steffi and Cooper). My sister, Michelle, would also give me little tidbits of information on the real people too (like they didn't get along, until someone told them to get it together because they had to work together ... now they are married and just had their first child in real life) but Cooper left (boo-hoo) and Steffi got involved with another really likeable fella, Tony (her bodyguard), then the murders happened ... and I really started to watch (well more at the tail end of the murders) then they [revamped the show as *The City*] ... and I haven't missed a day since (I even joined their mailing list).

The sets on *The City* are like no other soap, very wide open, interesting camera angles, great outdoor sequences (music video type) with shots of the real city all around ... I'm really enjoying it. (Although it's another ratings nightmare for me ... somehow—I don't know why—I always seem to like it better when the soaps are lower in the ratings, for example, Santa Barbara is another one I loved.)

The storylines move fast, Morgan Fairchild is always wearing some really fashionable clothing (sometimes really strange).

Joni Allen (Zoey) a young, former street person is a very interesting addition to the cast, she has a nose ring and pink hair (well, not in real life) and her pairing up with Australian Corey Paige (Richard) is a lot of fun to watch. Corey Paige is just magic to watch, he plays Morgan Fairchild's adopted son. Well, he thinks so anyway. He's been stealing scenes all over the place ... what a doll. He also tends to lean to the unique clothing items.

Roscoe Born ([formerly] of Santa Barbara ...) has been singing ...

it's nice just to have him back on daytime, but singing ... wow! Debbi Morgan (Angie) and Darnell Williams (Jacob), formerly of All My Children, are fantastic together, they have a really interesting story. Angie meets a man who looks exactly like her former husband, they fall in love with a few minor complications along the way (Angie's husband, Jacob's girlfriend). They decide to move to Soho, Jacob to open a bar with his friend Buck and Angie to open a clinic.

Another thing I noticed is that they cook in their kitchens, and have food in the refrigerator, and go to work (it's a little thing, but it's a nice thing).

A lot more than you wanted to know, eh? I'd better stop now, I could go on and on and on and on ... but if you ever want to see it let me know, my sister has tapes full of *The City.*

What do soaps tell us about ourselves?

When she was young, Audrey Roberts, a character on *CS,* had an illegitimate baby boy whom her parents insisted she give up for adoption. He was taken to Canada, where he grew up as Stephen Reid. In March 1996 Reid travelled to Weatherfield on business and visited his mother. While Audrey, her husband Alf, and daughter Gail knew of his existence, no one else in Weatherfield did, so residents were curious about him and his life in Canada. At the cafe Gail operated with Alma Baldwin, she described her brother, saying that he looked very fit.

Gail: He played ice hockey.

Alma: Well, they all do. Nothing else to do in winter.

After Alma meets him and pronounces him gorgeous, she muses, "You don't think of Canadians as sexy, all that ice ... And the Mounties with their pointy hats!"

Stephen even introduces Canadian politics. In explaining his business to Alf, he says that the Quebec sovereignty debate caused many businesses to leave Montreal for Toronto, where Stephen is based, and allowed Toronto to surpass Montreal as a business centre and become a more interesting city than it had been. He explains the name of his company, "Kbec," as "a way of saying thank you to the separatists"(March 13, 1996, episode).

So Canada gets a mention on *CS.*[92]

We also get occasional mention, and even Canadian location shoots, on American soaps. On *AW,* for instance, Grant and Vicky had a honeymoon from hell amidst the beautiful scenery of Lake Louise. Grant later was in Manitoba, but scenes (in a rustic hunting supply store) were all of interiors, not requiring a location shoot. American references to Canadian places can seem odd to Canadian ears; for example, Grant called to book a seat on "the next flight to Manitoba, Canada." And often when characters visit Canada, that is the only place-name ever given: "Canada," rarely the province or city.

These glimpses of ourselves we get on the soaps are not recognizably of *us:* they are of Canada as seen by non-Canadians. Despite increased Canadian television production, we see few images that reflect our reality. And as we absorb images from across the border, Alan Filewod warns, we should bear in mind that "we are seeing cultural values that originate from a very specific political and ideological system [that don't] necessarily reflect what's going on in our country" (interview).

Why is it imperative to have access to images that are home-grown, to see some version of one's own world reflected in continuing narrative form? Filewod summarized one reason why anglophone Canada needs a soap:

> Soap opera is the site of serious cultural reflection. And until a broad-caster makes the commitment, says that soap operas are important enough as a communicative vehicle, as a social vehicle, are so important in fact that we can't let the American multinational corporations control the terms of the discourse, control the vocabularies of them, then we'll never have one here. The overwhelming popularity of the soap operas suggests to me that they *are* important, they're deeply important to people; they really need to see them. (Interview)

In such a huge country as Canada, with a number of regions disparate in culture and outlook, a soap of the geographically rooted type that tells our regional stories would allow us to "know each other." I have in mind not just the "two solitudes" of Quebec and anglophone Canada, the most obvious cultural divide.[93] Nor do I think of the life of the "world class" megacity, Toronto, as showing Canadians our national culture. I may get involved in the stories and lives of the CBC's soap *Riverdale*, but even if it presented a "real looking" Toronto, I would agree with those I have heard say, "So what? It's *Toronto*. Who cares?" Living in the place that provides the butt of the ubiquitous "Newfie jokes" has sensitized me to the prejudices and lack of knowledge of my own region elsewhere in the country. My own stereotypes of the Prairies are of a place filled with cowboys and rabid gun-owners whose political agenda is worthy of the right-wing American National Rifle Association. I know neither the romantic nor the cynical stereotype is true to prairie culture and society, but what vehicles are there to (painlessly) educate me about that region? W.O. Mitchell television adaptations do not engage me in the world of western Canada intensively enough. Soaps, on the other hand, do offer sufficient inducement to large numbers of people; they engage us in the lives of others through long-term contact with characters whose circumstances may differ from our own, but whose joys and sorrows resonate in our own lives. Soap opera is an entertaining way of incorporating reflections and perspectives on the political and socio-cultural realities within which they themselves are based and viewed.

I can offer a strong case in point. In 1982 a current affairs radio soap, *Oil In The Family*, ran weekdays on CBC Radio Newfoundland from March until it was cancelled in June. Newfoundland had experienced the height of oil fever and tragic disillusionment following exploration of the Hibernia field off the Grand Banks. In the early hours of February 15, the Ocean Ranger drill rig sank in a storm, and all eighty men aboard were lost. The serial set issues of oil development, unemployment, rising house prices, and influx of outsiders within the context of the lives of a St. John's working-class family and their friends. It was immensely popular because it talked about what people on the street were talking about, in a witty and authentic way. Nor did it shy away from controversy; it outraged the Roman Catholic Church (very influential in Newfoundland) when the daughter, pregnant by her oil worker boyfriend, decided to have an abortion. Its willingness to tackle all realities, as they were happening, resulted in its cancellation, despite its popularity.

Oil in the Family was unusual in the annals of soap (or any radio drama) production not just for dealing with current affairs, but for dealing with them *on the day they were happening.* Not since the era of live radio or television production has story-based entertainment been so immediate. *Oil's* fifteen-minute script was mapped out in the morning based on the news, written, and taken to actors to rehearse in the afternoon. It aired late the same afternoon. Audience response logs indicated that many non-CBC listeners began tuning in for each day's episode (Chris Brookes, producer, personal communication). That suggests there is a place, and a desire, for stories that tell about the days of our (Canadian) lives.

Whether as controversy or fantasy, in a fictionalized Toronto's Riverdale district, a "real" Liverpool or a fictionalized Salford, "real" Los Angeles or fictionalized US eastern seaboard, soaps will continue allowing viewers to ignore the pressures of their own lives by watching someone else's for a while. They will allow us to appreciate our own happiness by sharing that of fictional characters. They will provide entertainment in the watching and the telling to friends over coffee in the kitchen or a modem hookup to cyberspace. Despite the oft-expressed fears for the death of the genre, soaps keep being introduced to the networks, cable stations, and, indeed, the internet. And the *grandes dames* of the genre continue, with periodic rough times, but they survive. So, too, will analysis of them. For as long as we want to know what happens next in the story, we are also going to want to know *why* we watch.

Appendix A:
Soaps' Most Daring Stories

SOD (September 3, 1991: 12-20) listed its choice of "Soaps' Most Daring Stories," as well as those that were "chickened out on." The daring social issue stories were

1.   (*SB*) "Eden's Rape": "The brutal crime of rape is a staple on daytime television.... The scene of the rape itself was unnerving and compelling to watch. Eden ... was shown experiencing a medical examination, answering probing questions about her intimate relationships, and attending draining therapy sessions. Her trauma was prolonged because her attacker tormented her with lewd phone calls.... [T]he culprit: Eden's gynecologist. Eden's assault and struggle to rebuild her life were realistic and poignant, and the brutal rape was never sensationalized.[94]

2.   (*B&B*) "Jake's Sexual Abuse": In this story, a man learned through therapy that his family problems and impotence stemmed from childhood sexual abuse by his uncle, a first for soap abuse stories in that the abuser was the same sex as the abused.

3.   (*AMC*) "Travis and Barbara's Bone Marrow Donor Baby": This problem presented the difficulties of finding a matching donor and explored the emotional difficulties for the parents, divorced and remarried to others, who decided to conceive another child in order to better their chances of a donor match. "Larkin Molloy's (Travis) departure forced the show to end this story conveniently (Travis and Barbara reunited; the baby was a perfect match) ..." First Lady Barbara Bush appeared on the show, to appeal for bone marrow donors.

4.   (*ATWT*) "Casey's Right-To-Die Story": Debilitated by Guillian-Barre syndrome, Casey lapsed into a coma. He did

not have time to write a living will, but his sister-in-law knew his wishes and withdrew his life support. Conflict within the family after her action was combined with exploration of "several sides of a controversial yet highly personal subject."

5. (*GH*) "Tom And Simone's Interracial Marriage": "The writers didn't shy away from showing the intimate side of the couple's loving relations. Viewers saw Tom and Simone together in bed and—shock!—they were seen kissing and caressing ... the pair confronted obstacles.... Tom overreacted and beat up a racist who insulted his wife, [forcing] him to examine his own prejudices ... When Tom had a one-night stand, Simone was angry, but the race of the other woman had nothing to do with it."[95]

In addition to those noted by *SOD*, I would include two more: first, a 1995 breast cancer story on *GH* that featured a long-term central character, Dr. Monica Quartermaine. It explored medical and emotional issues, presenting Monica's feelings of denial and her inability to accept support from husband and family, and dealt with treatment and her eventual mastectomy as well as the recurrence of a lump. The strain of the ordeal and her fear of being "less of a woman" were shown from her perspective and that of her worried but frustrated husband. The details of her recovery were realistically told and provided good advice to women. My second choice is *GH*'s exploration of rape in a 1998 story that paired a rape of a young girl by an unknown assailant, and Lucky Spencer's emotional support of her afterward, with Lucky's discovery of the circumstances—date rape—that brought his parents together. The story also delved into Luke's feelings of confusion and guilt both prior to and after Lucky confronted him. It continued with Luke and Laura confronting each other with their feelings about their past and their love for each other. In this story the issues were raised and interrogated from all perspectives, and done with some powerful acting from all the actors involved.

SOD continued its summary of risk-taking plots with "Stories that the Soaps Chickened Out On."

1. "AIDS without Horror": "Praise was heaped on *AMC* and *Y&R* when they wrote AIDS stories, but the finales were unrealistic. *AMC*'s Cindy and *Y&R*'s Jessica died what had to be the most painless AIDS deaths on record. No disfiguring lesions marred their lovely faces; numerous tubes and catheters weren't stuck into bodies racked with pain. Cindy and Jess just looked wan ... Makeup artists could have created effects to show how AIDS ravages its victims."[96]

2. "AIDS Without Death": "*AW* waffled by introducing Dawn Rollo, a young girl who hit town, came down with AIDS ... then left to spend her last days in Venice, Italy."

3. "Where's the Justice?": "*DOOL* focused on the serious problem of marital rape when Jack brutally attacked his wife, Kayla. Though she bravely filed charges, *DOOL* copped out when Jack got off via a plea bargain."

4. "The Bad Seeds": "*OLTL*'s Sarah became pregnant after she was raped ...; *ATWT*'s Shannon found herself with child after having sex with a man who turned out to be her uncle's murderer ... Both women conveniently miscarried, thus giving the writers noncontroversial solutions to the sticky problem of dealing with unwanted pregnancies."[97]

Notes

Notes to chapter one

1   See Allan 1995: 17-24 for discussion of "open" (i.e., British and American serials) with "closed" serials (i.e., Latin American *telenovelas*, etc.)

2   There are exceptions. Jay Hammer, who acted in *Texas,* the 1980–82 spin-off of *AW,* said that all stories were resolved by the final episode (interview). But three or four decades of story history would be more difficult to bring to a tidy end than *Texas's* two years.

        A spin-off is a show which is developed from another and generally includes one or more of the original cast's characters and perhaps some of the history and premises of the plotlines. *Texas* came from the fictional relocation of Iris Carrington Wheeler, an *AW* character, from Bay City to Texas where she made new friends whose stories provided material for continuing her saga. *Port Charles* is a spin-off, set in the same city and hospital as its originating soap, *General Hospital.* Prime-time shows also spin-off popular series: *Frasier* from *Cheers, The Jeffersons* from *All in the Family.*

3   Many researchers discuss the construction of narrative in soap opera as compared to traditional dramatic structure. See, for example, Archer 1992, Brown 1990, Modleski 1982, and Nochimson 1992, for discussion of dramatic forms and extended narrative in the soaps as a "feminine" form.

4   As we will see in later chapters, British serials enjoy rather more prestige than their North American counterparts.

5   The discussion is confined to the UK and US because elsewhere soaps are often intended as popular education devices. See Nariman (1993) for an examination of soap opera as a tool for education through entertainment, as developed by Miguel Sabido in Mexico. Also see Griffiths (1995) on the use of soap opera in teaching and preserving the Welsh language, Rofel (1995) on the use of melodrama in presenting a government-approved post-Tiananmen perspective on Chinese history and national identity, and Das (1995), Lutgendorf (1995), and

Gillespie (1995) on Hindu devotional serials. Abu-Lughod (1995) compares Egypt's "culture industry" use of soap opera as a method of popular education with the popularity in that country of the American import, *B&B*. See Cambridge (1992) for the use of radio soap opera for over forty years for purposes of education and development of African identity in Africa and the African diaspora. In the 1980s Sandinista-governed Nicaragua, government agencies and grass-roots community groups used "appropriate-technology" adaptations of soap operas for education in a land with few televisions by adapting the form to comic books and shows by popular theatre troupes. (see Brookes 1984).

6   American pre-eminence in exporting serials is being challenged by the phenomenal success of Brazil's TV-Globo and Mexico's Televisa, which, respectively, sell their serials to 100 and to 59 other nations (Allan 1995: 13).

7   Attention is not entirely lacking in the general media as well. The *Globe & Mail* periodically carries commentaries on soaps and articles about visiting actors, as does the *Toronto Star*. *Maclean's* in 1986 featured a cover promo entitled "Inside: The Rich and Sexy World of TV Soaps," discussing the industry and its fans in a three-page article. At the height of *GH*'s Luke-and-Laura fervour of the early 1980s, the actors appeared on the covers of several popular magazines. When they returned after a ten-year absence they were guests (in character) on the popular sitcom *Roseanne* (Roseanne and then husband Tom Arnold in turn appeared on *General Hospital*).

8   See Allen 1985, Cantor and Pingree 1982, Williams 1992, and Hagedorn 1995 for comprehensive histories of American soap operas from radio to television.

9   Hagedorn (1995: 36) reports that in 1940 there were 64 different soap operas on air, levelling off to 39 throughout the 1940s.

10   Procter and Gamble was an original sponsor of many soaps, and remains a leading sponsor today, with ownership of *AW*, *As the World Turns*, and *Guiding Light*. The other household products giant, Colgate-Palmolive, went out of the soap business when *The Doctors* was cancelled in 1982 (Cantor & Pingree 1983: 49).

11   "Similarly," Allen says, "western movies were called 'horse operas' in the 1930s" (1995: 4).

12   Although good and strong women predominated in all three types of radio soaps, all included male characters, good and bad, as well as bad women. Some, such as *Just Plain Bill*, featured men as central characters. Bill dispensed words of wisdom from his backyard just as Ma Perkins did from her kitchen table.

13   See Williams (1992: 171–78) and Nochimson (1992: 46–54) for discussion of radio soap heroines in terms of reality and/or fantasy compared to women's place in the American social structure. In reference to women's role in the Depression, Williams footnotes employment statistics and refers to a study of the "unreported" work and exchange of goods and services by which women of all classes helped each other and their families (1992: 209).

14   Cassata (1983: 87–88) summarizes Thurber's (1948) typology of soap characters in her comparison of radio and television soaps: (1) Homey Philosophers: *Ma Perkins, Just Plain Bill*; (2) Cinderellas: *Rags to Riches; Our Gal Sunday*; (3) Doctors and Nurses: *Woman in White, Young Doctor Malone*; (4) Young Women (unattached): *Single by Choice, The Romance of Helen Trent, Portia Faces Life*; (5) Men with Flexible Schedules; (6) Good People, Male and Female: living by a strict moral code that disallows "fun."

15   For this reason not all forecasted a shining future for television serials. Early commentators predicted that soaps would survive on radio but not television because watching *and* listening would be too disruptive of women's daily routine (Cantor & Pingree 1983: 47). Throughout the 1950s, however, soaps began to disappear from radio; the final four radio serials (including *Ma Perkins*) aired for the last time on November 25, 1960 (Cassata 1983: 85).

16   As of mid-1998, *AW* is currently very low in US ratings, and rumours abound that it will be cancelled. Its network, NBC, is bringing a new soap on board created by James Reilly, former head writer of *DOOL* and noted for his contribution of the "demonic possession" and other over-the-top stories of the mid-1990s. NBC may well axe the long-running *AW* in order to put its resources into its new project (*source:* e-mail discussion group posts from 1997 through mid-1998).

17   "Backburner" refers to plots or characters not centrally featured; "frontburner" refers to the dominant stories or characters.

18   Williams quotes Stedman's (1977) longer perspective on television programming in which he sees use of continuing narrative develop in the drama and comedy series of the 1960s and 1970s. In comparison with programs like *Alfred Hitchcock Presents*, series like *Bonanza* and, later, *All in the Family* showed "continuing characters in their 'continuing environment[s],' whether at home ... or at work" (1992: 33).

19   This information was obtained in an interview I conducted with Harry Elton in 1992.

Notes to chapter two

20   A sampling of these empirical studies follows: Estep and Macdonald (1985) compare crime rates on soaps with FBI statistics; Sutherland and Siniawsky (198) investigate "moral violations" (e.g., "There were 489 treatments of moral issues, 298 on 'All My Children' and 191 on 'General Hospital,' an average of 7.19 treatments per moral issue," 72.); Greenberg and D'Alessio (1985) inquire into sex (e.g., "Overall, there were 66 acts or references to acts of sexual intercourse (14 visual and 52 verbal), 17 of petting ... There was approximately 1.5 verbal mentions of intercourse in an hour," 313-14); Macdonald (1983) investigates frequency of use of drugs and alcohol, where viewers provided data on frequency, and Wallack et al. (1985) discusses alcohol in the context of its story, based on four and a half years of "observing" AMC; finally, Fine (1981) considers who talks to whom on soaps (e.g., "of the 232 conversations, 151 were male-female, 49 were female-female, and 32 were male-male," 100).

21   Williams ascribes T.W. Adorno's unwillingness to join Lazarsfeld's research team, which relied on quantitative methods, to his objections to the predominance of empiricism in American communications analysis. If Adorno's psychological and Marxist theoretical perspective had been combined with Lazarsfeld's approach she says,"the two social sciences, subjective and objective, might have been braided from the start ..." (1992: 9).

22   Carveth suggests there may be a perception of greater promiscuity among "viewers who watch a lot of soaps over a period of time and who do not attend church" (1992: 14).

23   Noam Chomsky (1994), notably, has explored the ways news reporting is shaped by political or economic agendas that influence what is considered newsworthy and how it is presented.

24   Dr. Berg was the New York psychiatrist who declared that soap viewing was harmful to the health on the basis of data recording only *his* reactions.

25   See Gluckman (1959) for an anthropological view of the role of "rituals of reversal" as allowing dissension to be expressed as a means of maintaining an uneasy balance between social groups essentially at odds with each other; and Brookes (1988) for a history of Christmas "mummering" in Newfoundland as a ritual of reversal with potential for political change and/or social upheaval, and the 1970s borrowing of the term, and concepts, in developing popular political theatre in Newfoundland. See also a discussion of the popularity of *Y&R* in Trinidad, where it is seen as embodying "bacchanal" or social disorder associated with Carnival (Miller 1995).

26   James Thurber in 1948 saw something akin, although a mirror image, in the radio soaps: he believed they portrayed men as emasculated, as few in number and/or disabled, and women as the dominant and competent tenders of family and community. He considered this to have a pernicious effect on American males. Brown looks on the flip side, considering that soaps confer on women a decided benefit: a kind of secret code. Both see similar social agendas hidden in simple domestic entertainment; but how differently they interpret and evaluate them.

27   As well as what women do when they discuss the soaps with other fans.

28   In chapter five I discuss the precise ways in which British soaps reflect British cultural structures, and specifically social and geographical place. Here I will present simply one, intriguing, analysis of British soaps.

29   In fact, in all British serials, strong women and matters of community and emotional relationships generally outweigh social or political matters. It can be argued, however, that this is because soaps, even in the demographically more mixed British audiences, are primarily directed to women, who understandably want to see strong female characters as well as stories that are relevant to their lives.

30   Even the "teaching storylines" increasingly common on American soaps are intended merely to educate people about social or medical issues. Most seem more akin to public service announcements than to ideological debates in that audiences are told, with less or more subtlety, what the appropriate belief or response should be.

31   Ironically (from a North American standpoint), much of the British analytic criticism of British serials, especially *CS*, focuses on its unreality (see Geraghty 1981; Jordan 1981; Lovell 1981). See especially chapters four and six.

Notes to chapter three

32   Cantor and Pingree give a concise description of the creation of American soaps from production decisions to acting. They provide potted biographies of key people in the creation of the genre: Frank and Anne Hummert, who created and refined radio soaps, and Irna Phillips, who went from radio soap writing to creating television soaps, including *GL*, *AW*, *ATWT*, and *DOOL* (1983: 57–67,40–44). Intintoli (1992) also outlines the industry and production process in his study of *GL*. Finally, Paterson (1981) describes the production methods used in *CS* and examines its narratives in light of its production technology.

33   When it does succeed, this needn't be because audiences simply resign themselves to the rupture. Audience reaction is rather more complex

than that. Whether abrupt change is embraced or not also has to do with differences in the way individual fans "read" the soaps and the soap industry. The expectations and motivations of fans are discussed in chapter six. Here, the point is that an audience's attitude towards continuity and change is shaped by micro (individual) as well as macro (national, cultural) factors.

34 As well, of course, as in origins. The different early histories of British and American soaps were discussed in chapter one.

35 Between Manchester and Liverpool, for example, there is considerable cultural similarity, yet their respective residents seem to regard them as akin to East and West Berlin before the wall came down. Before I left Manchester for Liverpool, three elderly Percy Sugden-like gentlemen warned me about the perils of Liverpool, and were relieved I was not driving a car: "They'd take four tires off, they'd take wheels and all, first time you left it!" In Liverpool people were surprised that I had survived Manchester, and considered me to be a lunatic with a death-wish to have walked around it *alone*. And in Leeds, Liverpool and Manchester are thought of as Sodom and Gomorrah with pitiable football teams.

Though Canadians are not regionalist in this sense—there is no particular historical animosity between, say, Atlantic Canada and the Prairies—there is an interesting parallel between British and Canadian regionalism in their attitudes towards their respective "premier cities." One reason Toronto is unlikely to succeed as a setting for a national soap is that people who don't live there dislike the city and all it stands for; they don't want to hear more about it. In this, Canadians are more like Britons than like Americans. Non-Londoner Britons make no bones about the fact that London is not the hub of their universe (though perhaps residents of Kansas or Idaho feel similarly about New York and Los Angeles, but are just not so ferociously vocal about it).

36 See Geraghty (1995) and Buckingham (1987) for analysis of *Brookside* and *EE*.

37 The village was built in the mountains of Spain, but seaside location shots were done in a resort town on the coast (Ayres, interview).

38 UK daytime serials do not attract the viewers or analytic respect the prime-time serials receive. Perhaps because daytime programming has a relatively short history in the UK and, as in the US, is associated with fluff, the daytime serials have respectable viewership numbers, but nothing like the prime-time ones. An afternoon (national) airtime was given as one reason why English viewers and analysts dismissed a Scottish Television soap, *Take the High Road*. They also mentioned the difficulty of understanding the accent. Perhaps it was a fluke, but the

central storyline while I was watching in England was about a funeral for a village child, certainly not a cheerful topic.

39   These quotations are extracted from interviews I conducted with Harry Elton, who lives in Ottawa, in late 1991 and with Tony Warren several months later (March 1992) in Manchester.

40   The Canadian "Street" newsletter (No. 18, 1992) wrote: "'DOOMED' sang the headline in a 1960 edition of Britain's *Daily Mirror.* Subject? *Coronation Street*'s first episode. Journalist Ken Irwin blundered on: 'There is little reality in this new serial ... The programme is doomed from the outset.' Thirty-two years later, Ken has climbed down red-faced. 'My only excuse ... is that I was a young and rather naive critic ...What can I say except sorry?'"

41   For an analysis of soap stories informed by the author's experiences as a writer on several American soaps, see Nochimson (1992).

42   In April 1998, the firing of Charles Keating, who played Carl Hutchins, upset *AW* fans so much that many boycotted sponsor Procter & Gamble's products, with the names of P&G products circulated on email newsgroups such as *ratsm. SOD* wondered if fan displeasure was responsible for a noticeable drop in the show's ratings (April 28, 1998: 11).

43   Hence the practice of many fans who videotape their stories so that they can fast forward through scenes that are not of interest to them.

44   Throughout the first half of 1998, *AW* e-mail fans grew so dispirited about the many unpopular changes in storylines and characters that many ceased their campaigning to keep the show on the air. Previously vociferously activist fans said they no longer cared if the show was cancelled.

45   The reader can find a study of music, costumes, sets, and so on in Cassata and Skills 1983.

46   The following quotations are from a personal interview with O'Rourke and McCann. March 1992.

47   In January 1993 the English tabloids reported that the whole *Lifeboys* enterprise had failed.

48   In years of reading American soap magazines, I have seldom seen an actor criticized for speaking in an accent, real or assumed, inconsistent with her/his supposed origins. Canadian viewers, or at least those who watch *CS,* can be more demanding about such details: I've read many e-mail messages from Canadians unhappy about an appearance on that show of an actor with an obvious American accent portraying a Canadian character.

49   As I mentioned above, *CS* expanded to four times a week in 1996. This move was not seen as wise by all. In 1992 Bill Tarmey (Jack Duck-

worth) told me he did not think the quality could be maintained if the show went to four times weekly. In May 1996 he was mentioned on *CS*'s e-mail group as having said he did not like the idea, but had no plans to leave the show.

Notes to chapter four

50   Playing two characters is a common device on American soap operas. It allows writers to develop the melodramatic intrigue of mistaken identity and gives actors a chance to strut their stuff, to show their acting range liberated from the confines of one character. There is usually a "good" and an "evil" twin.

51   This does not make explicit mention of what I think is the crucial reason the reprised roles worked: the characters'/actors' *enormous* popularity. When Geary took on the role of Bill Eckhart many fans were happy just to have him back.

52   It's worth noting that chemistry can work the other way as well. When one of a pair of memorable actors (Geary and Francis; *DOOL*'s Deirdre Hall and Wayne Northrup; more recently, *DOOL*'s Peter Reckell and Kristian Alfonso [Bo and Hope]) reprises his or her daytime roles, usually that presages the return of the other actor. But even when fans and writers may want the reunion of a couple, other forces can intervene. In its gossip section, *SOD* says of a certain duo: "[They were] very popular a few years back, but when the half who still remains on the show was asked how he/she would feel if the other half returned, the star said he/she would in fact mind *very much*. Consequently, the other half will not be returning" (May 7, 1996: 82).

53   The way of handling real-life death varies from show to show. From the inception of *DOOL* until his death in 1994, Macdonald Carey portrayed Dr. Tom Horton, and he introduced the show with these words: "Like sands through the hourglass, so are the days of our lives. I'm Macdonald Carey and this is the Days of Our Lives." The producers evidently decided to honour his memory by continuing to use his first line (omitting his second, in which he introduced himself). Soon after Carey's death in 1994, his character, Dr. Tom Horton, died while attending meetings out of town. All of *DOOL*'s Salem, actors and viewers, mourned the loss of the family patriarch and original cast member. Butler gives another example of how real death is handled: the death of actor Don MacLaughlin and the parallel death of his *ATWT* character Chris Hughes, in which "a memorial was chromakeyed over the shot of the framed photograph [of MacLaughlin/Hughes]: 'Don MacLaughlin, 1906–1986.' In so doing, the death of

MacLaughlin was elided with the death of the character ... Was the photograph wholly within the fiction (Chris Hughes) or was it a signifier of 'reality' (Don MacLaughlin)?" (Butler 1995: 145).

By contrast, *CS*'s Ena Sharples moved away to keep house for a small-town vicar when her portrayer, Violet Carson, retired. When Ms. Carson died, no mention was made on the show. In the fictional world of Weatherfield, we may take comfort in thinking that Ena is still happily bullying her poor vicar.

54 Fletcher Reade, and Jay Hammer, were written out of *GL* in early 1998. Hammer is quoted in *Soap Opera News* about his fourteen years on *GL:* "It's gratifying and touching to know ... that I've managed to entertain so many people consistently ... they felt they got value received" (March 3, 1998: 45). (He was referring to letters and calls from fans, and even a website established about him.)

55 Until recent years, many American soaps did not include the names of actors in the credits. Best boys, gaffers, and assistants to the assistant had their names displayed daily, but actors at best got credit at the close of the Friday episode. Even when cast lists were scrolled, the only actors singled out were long-time patriarchs and matriarchs. On *DOOL,* Macdonald Carey and Frances Reid (Dr. Tom and Mrs. Alice Horton) were the only ones who received special billing until the return of Hall and Northrup. Beverlee Mackenzie, around whom the 1980s *AW* spin-off *Texas* was created, received star billing.

56 Stefano is the off-and-on long-standing villain of *DOOL.* He is very wealthy from his criminal activities, but we rarely see him engaging in business dealings. His adopted son, Peter Blake, took over the day-to-day operation of Stefano's prostitution and drug-running enterprises. Peter's sister and Stefano's adopted daughter is Kristen, ex-wife of Stefano's biological son (therefore her adoptive brother) Tony, which may lead to all manner of speculation on the soap opera-acceptable definition of incest. Stefano himself has returned from the dead enough times to make a cat blush.

57 When I was editing a taped broadcast for CBC Radio about the soaps, I played the theme music of *Y&R.* A technician came in and immediately said, "That's *Y&R!*" He denied ever watching the show, but knew the music well enough to immediately recognize it.

58 Davidson eventually ended up playing five parts: Kristen Blake, Kristen's look-alike Susan, Susan's twin sister, Susan's brother, and another sister, Penelope, who, I think, was found dead in a swimming pool. I lost track of this story, but gained respect for Davidson's ability to pull off such a convoluted plot, which was the finale for her April 1998 departure from *DOOL.* Since only one of her multiple charac-

ters actually died, she, like Stefano, may return. I hope so.

59   Northrup was not available to reprise the role as he had moved to a role on *Port Charles*. No mention of the physical difference in "Roman" was made, surprising in a show that relies so much on plastic surgery for its storylines.

60   Amanda had a sudden growth spurt, going from age eight to eighteen in about a year. This phenomenon is termed SORAS (Soap Opera Rapid Aging Syndrome) in the industry magazines and in e-mail groups. Tom Eplin (Jake on *AW*) joked about this in reference to Amanda at a Toronto public appearance in 1991: "Beware when a child is sent upstairs to do her homework; a year later she'll come back downstairs as Miss Illinois." (Kitchen and Bath Show, Mississauga).

61   Timmins's siblings are in the music group Cowboy Junkies.

62   Michael Zaslow died Deceember 6, 1998, of Lou Gehrig's disease. He had played Roger Thorpe on *GL* until his illness was diagnosed. Let go from that show, he was hired on *OLTL*, where he played a character suffering from the same disease.

63   *SOD* predictors could not have imagined then that in late 1998 Hope would still be trying to find out who she really is—whether she is indeed Hope Williams Brady or the mysterious Gina, victim or collaborator of Stefano.

64   Because his appearances were so brief, Frisco's behaviour seemed irresponsible in the extreme: he would return, influence the course of events in various ways, and then disappear, leaving others to deal with the repercussions. For example, after one sweeps week, he left his ex-wife pregnant with their second child. His lengthy disappearances also made him seem a negligent father, despite the gravity of his position as an intelligence officer with the WSB, an American security agency.

65   Bet's earrings are her trademark, along with her white-blonde hair piled up in curls to the ceiling. Her earrings, large and jewelled, are available at the *CS* giftshop at Granada Studios. Beverlee McKenzie, as Iris Cory Carrington Wheeler on *AW*, was closest to Bet in appearance among American actors.

Notes to chapter five

66   There was an early recast of Bet's step-granddaughter Vicky and a 1997 recast of a teenaged Nick Tilsley. Producer Brian Park's replacement of the previous, ordinary-looking Nick with a very good-looking young "hunk" gave many viewers further evidence of Park's "Americanizing" of *CS* (e-mail discussion).

67   See discussion in chapter one.

68   Here I glide over the point that advertising operates not just by pro-
      viding information, but by manipulating emotion, for insofar as the
      latter is involved, advertisements fall under the rubric of "normative
      appeal," addressed in the following paragraphs.

69   Their treatment of issues is also, of course, influenced by the "slant" or
      emphasis of the particular show. *CS* and *Emmerdale* emphasize tradi-
      tional humour and community over explicit topical items; *EE* is
      explicitly urban in its emphasis; and all British serials are more apt than
      American ones to raise an issue, present all the sides, and leave viewers
      to make their own judgements. Says *Brookside's* Mal Young: "I try and
      keep away from the word 'educating' because ... I'm not setting myself
      up to be a social worker.... But viewers know that when they come to
      us, they're gonna be made to think.... The thing that I like to frustrate
      people with is that there aren't these easy answers.... We're sometimes
      called 'Miseryside' [a play on Liverpool's nickname "Merseyside"]
      because ... no matter what the story is, if it's real we'll put it on the
      screen, even if it's really miserable" (interview). American soaps, by
      contrast, tend to present a situation and then give counsel on the best
      way to deal with it, without delving into all sides of the issue.

70   For more extensive discussion of these issues and their presentation in
      American soaps see, for example, Williams (1992: 95-126), Nochimson
      (1992: 161-92), Geraghty (1995), and Fuqua (1995).

71   Williams notes a rare exception: "One day in early 1988, *Santa Barbara's*
      hero, Cruz Castillo (A Martinez) was protecting a democratic Central
      American leader who had come to Santa Barbara for a secret meeting.
      Musing while waiting to outwit the bombers and double/triple covert
      agents, Cruz came close to scorning American imperialism and inter-
      ference in 'people's' governance" (1992: 99). A very brave exception,
      considering the political climate of the time!

72   One notable exception was the 1995 *GH* plot involving Robin
      (Kimberley McCullough), who grew up on *GH*, and her boyfriend,
      Stone. Stone, a relatively new but very popular young character, devel-
      oped full-blown AIDS and died; the story took centre stage and
      unfolded over most of a year. One viewer responded: "No one has ever
      developed a story as important as the teen AIDS storyline on GH. It's
      timely and significant [and] could do no more to alert teens to the pre-
      sent dangers of AIDS.... [D]espite my love for Robin, I think the most
      valuable thing GH could do for society is to have Robin test HIV-pos-
      itive (S.B., Daly City, CA, quoted in *SOD* 20, 21: October 10, 1995:
      74-75). Robin did test positive, but she is living a full life without ever
      forgetting the realities of her health needs.

73   Ironically, perhaps, Brian Park did introduce environmental protection

issues into *CS* during his tenure as producer in 1997 and early 1998. He created the new, and rather one-dimensional character of Spyder, a young man whose principal storyline was a rather buffoonish tale of "direct action" to save a stand of trees from developers. He and his band of local, newly recruited eco-warriers then moved on to target the local supermarket's selling of Norwegian products in protest against Norway's continued whaling industry. These stories, which included Spyder's elderly aunt Emily Bishop (a long-time character), were presented in a caricatured manner doing justice to neither the issues or the characters.

74   See chapter two for discussion and citations of studies of the "cultivation effect" school of thought.

75   Actors' decisions to stay or leave and the "chemistry" between them also influence the pairing and breaking-up of couples. Because soap opera weddings are usually glorious extravaganzas, attracting large audiences, they have been used to boost ratings of slipping shows or to attract large numbers during the ratings May and September "sweep" periods.

76   Luke and Laura of *GH* are an interesting exception. Aside from the bad-guy arch-enemy stories that have bracketed several of their stints on *GH,* their ongoing drama lay in their marriage. Their troubles and character development have largely been multi-sided and realistic, not simply connected to their relationship; they have not always been beset by exotic dilemmas and unlikely twists of fate. Laura has been endangered by her involvement in community efforts to stop undesirable (and usually mob-backed) development. Luke, while trying to be a responsible businessman, has had friendships and his marriage damaged by his business arrangement and friendship with Sonny, the man who secretly took over Frank Smith's criminal empire after his (presumed final) death. None of these are entirely unlike the trials and tribulations viewers might face in their lives; though dramatically heightened, they are not presented in a standard, one-dimensional melodramatic form. The Luke-and-Laura storylines remained multi-faceted and fresh, even when their marriage was going well. It may be the abilities of the actors or the attention paid to writing for them. In the spring of 1998, their marital history became a major front-burner story, even with Genie Francis (Laura) gone. See chapter four and Appendix A for a discussion of the date rape episode.

77   A case in point: Dimitri, an ex-husband of *AMC* diva Erica Kane, left her because of her addiction to pain-killers. This led to an explicit "teaching" storyline in which she underwent treatment at the Betty Ford Clinic. After overcoming her denial, and anger at not being

treated like the diva she believed herself to be, she succeeded in overcoming her problem. Afterward she proclaimed, and explained, the value of the twelve-step program at every possible opportunity.

78   For the edification of non-soap watchers who roll their eyes about the weird names soap characters have, I point out that "Stone" is a street nickname the character preferred to his real name of Michael. However, with the existence of "Ridge" and "Thorne" on *B&B*, there is validity to the point!

79   Adrienne was played by Judi Evans Luciano who now plays the strong and gutsy Paulina on *AW.* This casting goes against the type of her previous soap roles.

80   In his machismo overprotectiveness towards his younger sister, his large, close family, and his cooking abilities, Joe Carlino represents just about every Italian stereotype that exists. If this were a Hispanic or black character, probably there would be criticism of such pigeonholing. However, Joe Barbara plays his role of Joe Carlino with panache, so maybe that softens the impact.

81   Characters are rarely seen actually working. Presumably, as writer Tom Elliott said of discussions about elections, etc., on *CS,* they work during the twenty-three hours of the day when we are not watching them. However, their lack of involvement in work can stretch credibility: in 1997 an e-mail fan figured that *DOOL*'s Jack and Jennifer must have been replaced as co-hosts of their television talk show, since they had not appeared at work, or even mentioned it, in many months. Perhaps mention of their jobs seemed to writers to be an unimportant distraction from the adventure of their front-burner story. Many fans, however, want those details for plausibility.

Notes to chapter six

82   Porter puts the point in a way that implies greater distance than I would generally impute to soap fans—his use of "patronizingly" is telling.

83   The role of soap opera viewing in providing material for "gossip," especially in terms of its form of "feminine discourse" in multiple and overlapping narrative as well as its female-oriented (real or ideal) perspective, has been extensively discussed in the literature; see Hobson (1990), Brown (1990), and Modleski (1982) for examples of different approaches to this topic.

84   Since videotapes can be kept, they can be loaned to those who missed episodes. E-mail user groups are filled with plaintive messages such as "I missed that episode, could anyone send me a tape?"

85   The technology of VCRs, by allowing greater control over our circumstances of viewing, strengthens the ritualistic aspects of that viewing and supports the view of soaps as adult "cuddle literature" (Porter 1977: 782).

86   Shows and actors have internet homepages, some established by the shows or networks and others by fans as tributes to their favourite soaps or actors. There are "chat rooms" and other interactive web fora where fans and industry personnel can talk through cyberspace with each other. There are also email discussion groups, some open to anyone with access to newsgroups and others which are by subscription (no fee is involved, but one must sign up in order to receive and send messages to the list membership). The most accessible, and very entertaining, email groups are in *rec.arts.tv.soaps*: *rats* for short. All the networks are featured: *rats.cbs* for CBS, *rats.a* for ABC, *rats.n* for NBC, and others. British serials have their own homepages and discussion groups, either under the *rec.arts* heading, *alt.tv*, or subscription lists.

87   Though to some this seems not too slim a basis for starting a relationship. "I'm breaking up with my boyfriend," one soap fan wrote, "solely on the basis that he hates watching soaps. And I met somebody online.... What can I say? We started a conversation about General Hospital and the rest is history. Funny how life works, eh?" (T., rats.m, May 26, 1996).

88   Soap audience analyses and descriptions exist in all the single-author monographs on soap opera cited in the References to this volume, and in most of the edited monographs. The empiricist studies of audiences cited in chapter two relied on university student audiences.

89   That viewer saw soaps as allowing her to vent her feelings, permitting malicious pleasure without harming anyone, and so improving her moral character: "I've become a much nicer person in real life" (*SOD*, April 9, 1996: 58). People do get very worked up about storylines. Here's a 1996 *rats* e-mail discussion about an *AW* story in which Felicia discovers her lover's estranged wife and his brother *in flagrante delicto*: *Ly*: If Faux-licia gets on Sharlene's case for this, I'll reach right into my TV screen and rip her little fictional face right off'n her fictional head. The nerve ... to walk right into someone's bedroom without even knocking! Let's hear nothing more about Shrewlene's bad manners, shall we? oh, my, I am livid. *puff*puff*wheeze*.
      Li: Uh-oh, I definitely see people entering the "Hypocrites are us" zone. Ok, Felicia was wrong to just go in the bedroom. But gotcha!!!!! Now the shoe is on the other foot, and Michael is acting true to form, with don't-tell-John, etc. Sharlene has played being caught cool so far. But Michael: tsk, tsk. Sort of what's good for the goose (John) is good

for the gander (Sharlene). At any rate they are both still married and have thus committed adultery. One question does come to mind. I know that John & Felicia care for one another. But does Michael care for Sharlene the same way, or was this just a blowing-off-steam type of f★ck?

90   *The Nanny* has had further links to the soap world. The male lead in the series is Charles Shaughnessy, formerly Shane Donavon on *AMC,* and star and executive producer Fran Drescher has had several soap actors appear on the show, including Eric Braeden (Victor, *Y&R*) and Stephen Nichols (Stefan, *GH*).

91   Her message itself illustrates both the willingness of soap fans to chat and the breadth of the e-mail reach: she contacted me about the Canadian prime-time series *Due South* after I had introduced myself, and my interest in soaps, to a non-soap e-mail list group.

92   And *CS* gets a certain amount of disapproving e-mail from Canadians, for the actor who played Stephen Reid had an *American* accent.

93   Note, however, that Quebec has its own stories that speak to itself: its *teleromans*. These are very popular, although so too are American soaps, led by *AW* (Novakovitch, interview).

Notes to appendix a

94   The presentation of rape on soaps often provokes viewer outrage. Too often the horror of the act is not presented, or it is a plot device to bring characters together or break them up, or the rapist is "redeemed." As an example, a letter to *SOD* asks about a long-ago rape on *ATWT*: "Josh raped Iva, and Lily was the result. So why is everyone so nice to Josh now? How was he vindicated of such a heinous crime?" (LAT, Chicago, IL, 17: 25: Dec. 8, 1992: 136). Williams (1992: 109-12) discusses what she quotes a fan as calling "Kayla's magic" in refashioning a rapist and kidnapper as a model loving husband on *DOOL*. Most shows have at least one redeemed rapist. Other types of villains are also redeemed, but, in discussions I've had with fans, it is most often the incidence of rape which stand out in their minds. "Redemption" usually comes about if the actor/character becomes popular with fans, despite his (in the case of rapists) criminal action. Fans do not forget, however much they like the character in his new incarnation. That is why so many were pleased to see the history of *GH*'s Luke and Laura's relationship, including the date-rape, addressed after twenty years.

95   To the best of my knowledge, interracial romances on soaps usually

feature a black woman and a white man, the less-threatening pairing in American (male) mythology. *AMC* broke the pattern by pairing dread-locked "hunk" Noah with Julia Santos. Noah, cast as the "angry black man," at one point thought Julia's to reluctance to move friendship to romance was due to his colour. *Y&R* followed up by teaming first Nathan and then his brother-in-law Malcolm, both black, with white Keesha. Keesha subsequently died of an AIDS-related illness, con-tracted from a former (white) lover and passed the virus on to Nathan, thereby placing his wife and son at risk of infection. AIDS, marital infidelity, and family loyalties were the bones of contention here, not the colour of the people involved. I cannot help but wonder if it is significant that both Julia and Keesha are olive-complexioned brunettes instead of the ubiquitous blondes of soapland. A student in the summer of 1998 told me she noticed that Victoria's (*Y&R*) blonde hair began to get darker when she began dating Neil, a black man, and she wondered if this was in response to the angry reaction some view-ers have had to the pairing. For example, a letter to *SOD*: "Please, please, please don't pair black and white. I have black friends, so I'm not biased. I just don't think the races should be intimate" (*SOD*: June 23, 1998:5).

96   *Y&R* did not take *SOD*'s advice. In spring 1996 Keesha (a minor char-acter) died a painless, "wan-looking" death. She was hospitalized with pneumonia, but that seemed to be the only side-effect she developed, and she collapsed a couple of times in her apartment, supposedly in great pain. Also, in a show with very slow-moving plots, she learned she might be infected, tested positive, developed full-blown AIDS, and died, all within a matter of months. Her infection was apparently a device for causing strife between two other characters.

97   There has been some improvement here. In 1995 on *AMC,* Julia was raped by a drug dealer and became pregnant. Possible AIDS infection was discussed, and her decision to have an abortion was explored in several ways. Her Roman Catholic family was horrified, although eventually one sister agreed to support her throughout the ordeal. And, at a time when American abortion clinics were being attacked by anti-abortion activists, she had to make her way through a crowd of violent protestors. Even some of her acquaintances were among the protestors, causing argument and counter-argument and discussion within the group about the appropriateness of violence as a tactic to preserve life. The counselling procedure and the stance of doctors who perform abortions was represented by including Julia's physician sister in the process.

References

Books, Articles, Archival Sources

Abu-Lighod, Lila. (1995). The objects of soap opera: Egyptian television and the cultural politics of modernity. In *Worlds Apart*. Ed. Daniel Miller. London: Routledge.

Allen, Robert C. (1985). *Speaking of soap operas.* Chapel Hill, NC: University of North Carolina Press.

___. (Ed.). (1995). *To be continued: Soap operas around the world.* London: Routledge.

Archer, Jane. (1992). The fate of the subject in the narrative without end. In *Staying Tuned...* Ed. Suzanne Frentz. Bowling Green, OH: Bowling Green State University Popular Press.

Arnheim, Rudolf. (1944/1979). The world of the daytime serial. In *Radio research 1942-43.* Ed. P. Lazarsfeld and F. Stanton. New York: Arno Press.

Badsen, G.T. (1966/1938). *Niger Ibos: A description of the primitive customs and animistic beliefs etc. of the Ibo people of Nigeria.* London: Frank Cass.

Baldwin, Kate. (1995). Montezuma's revenge: Reading "Los Ricos También Lloran" in Russia. In *To be continued...* Ed. Robert C. Allen. London: Routledge.

Belenky, Mary Field, et al. (1986). *Women's ways of knowing: The development of self, voice, and mind.* New York: Basic Books.

Brookes, Chris. (1984). *Now we know the difference: The people of Nicaragua.* Toronto: NC Press.

___. (1988). *A public nuisance: A history of the Mummers Troupe.* St. John's: Institute for Social and Economic Research, Memorial University of Newfoundland.

Brown, Mary Ellen. (1990). Motley moments: Soap operas, carnival, gossip and the power of the utterance. In *Television and women's culture.* Ed. Mary Ellen Brown. London: Sage.

Buckingham, David. (1987). *Public secrets: EastEnders and its audience.* London: British Film Institute.

Buckman, Peter. (1984). *All for love: A study in soap opera.* New York: Salem House.

Butler, Jeremy G. (1995). "I'm not a doctor, but I play one on TV": Characters, actors and acting in television soap opera. In *To be continued...* Ed. Robert C. Allen. London: Routledge.

Calhoun-French, Diane M. (1992). Soaps and serials: The transformation of daytime drama into romance literature. In *Staying tuned...* Ed. Suzanne Frentz. Bowling Green, OH: Bowling Green State University Popular Press.

Cambridge, Vibert C. (1992). Radio soap operas in global Africa: Origins, applications, and implications. In *Staying tuned...* Ed. Suzanne Frentz. Bowling Green, OH: Bowling Green State University Popular Press.

Cantor, Muriel, and Suzanne Pingree. (1983). *The soap opera.* Beverly Hills: Sage.

Carveth, Rodney A. (1992). Exploring the effects of "love in the afternoon": Does soap opera viewing create perceptions of a promiscuous world? In *Staying tuned...* Ed. Suzanne Frentz. Bowling Green, OH: Bowling Green State University Popular Press.

Cassata, Mary. (1983). The more things change, the more they are the same: An analysis of soap operas from radio to television. In *Life on Daytime Television.* Ed. Mary Cassata and Thomas Skills. Norwood, NJ: Ablex.

Cassata, Mary, and Thomas Skills. (Eds.). (1983). *Life on daytime television: Tuning-in American serial drama.* Norwood, NJ: Ablex.

Crofts, Stephen. (1995). Global neighbours? In *To be continued....* Ed. Robert C. Allen. London: Routledge.

Das, Veena. (1995). On soap opera: What kind of anthropological object is it? In *Worlds Apart.* Ed. Daniel Miller. London: Routledge.

Davidson, Joy. (1991). *The soap opera: The drive for drama and excitement in women's lives.* New York: Berkeley. (Originally published 1988 by Jeremy P. Thatcher/St. Martin's Press, under the title *The Agony of It All*)

Dyer, Richard. (1981). "Introduction." In *Coronation Street.* Ed. Richard Dyer et. al. Television Monograph 13. London: British Film Institute.

Estep, Rhoda, and Patrick T. Macdonald. (1985). Crime in the afternoon: Murder and robbery on soap operas. *Broadcasting & Electronic Media* 29(3): 323–31.

Fine, Marlene G. (1981). Soap opera conversations: The talk that binds. *Journal of Communication* 31(3): 97–107.

Frentz, Suzanne (Ed.). (1992). *Staying tuned: Contemporary soap opera criticism.* Bowling Green, OH: Bowling Green State University Popular Press.

Friedan, Betty. (1963). *The feminine mystique.* New York: Dell.

Fuqua, Joy V. (1995). "There's a queer in my soap!": The homophobia/AIDS story-line of *One Life to Life.* In *To be continued...* Ed. Robert C. Allen. London: Routledge.

Geraghty, Christine. (1995). Social issues and realist soaps: A study of British soaps in the 1980/1990s. In *To be continued...* Ed. Robert C. Allen. London: Routledge.

Gerbner, G., and L. Gross (1976). Living with television: The violence profile. *Journal of Communication* 26: 172–99.

Gillespie, Marie. (1995). Sacred serials, devotional viewing, and domestic worship: A case-study in the interpretation of two TV versions of "The Mahabharata" in a Hindu family in west London. In *To be continued...* Ed. Robert C. Allen. London: Routledge.

Gilligan, Carol. (1982). *In a different voice.* Cambridge, MA: Harvard University Press.

Gluckman, Max. (1959). The licence in ritual. In *Custom and conflict in Africa.* Glencoe, IL: Free Press.

Greenberg, Bradley S., and Dave D'Alessio. (1985). Quantity and quality of sex in the soaps. *Journal of Broadcasting & Electronic Media* 29(3): 309–21.

Griffiths, Alison. (1995). National and cultural identity in a Welsh-language soap opera. In *To be continued...* Ed. Robert C. Allen. London: Routledge.

Gzowski, Peter. (1975). Interview with Kate Reid. *Gzowski on FM.* CBC Radio Archives, Toronto.

Haley, Alex. (1976). *Roots.* New York: Dell.

Haskell, Molly. (1973). *From reverence to rape: The treatment of women in the movies.* New York: Holt, Rinehart & Winston.

Herman, Edward S., and Noam Chomsky. *Manufacturing Consent: the political economy of mass media.* New York: Pantheon Books, 1988.

Hobson, Dorothy. (1990). Women audiences and the workplace. In *Television and women's culture: The politics of the popular.* Ed. Mary Ellen Brown. London: Sage.

Hoggart, Richard. (1957). *The Uses of Literacy.* London: Chatto & Windus, 1971.

Intintoli, Michael J. (1984). *Taking soaps seriously: Guiding Light.* New York: Praeger Special Studies.

Jordan, Marion. (1981). Realism and Convention. In *Coronation Street.* Ed. Richard Dyer et al. London: British Film Institute.

Kay, Graeme. (1990). *The Coronation Street Quiz Book.* London: Boxtree.

LaGuardia, Robert. (1983). *Soap world: Ma Perkins to Mary Hartman.* New York: Arbor House.

Levi-Strauss, C. (1967). *Structural anthropology.* Trans. C. Jacobsen and B.G. Schepf. Garden City, NY: Doubleday.

Leith-Ross, Sylvia. (1939/1965). *African women: A study of the Ibo of Nigeria.* London: Routledge & Kegan Paul.

Little, Daran, and Hill, Bill. *Weatherfield life.* Salford: Granada Television.

Lovell, Terry. (1981). Ideology and *Coronation Street.* In *Coronation Street.* Ed. Richard Dyer et al. London: British Film Institute.

Lutgendorf, Philip. (1995). All in the (Raghu) family: A video epic in cultural context. In *To be continued...* Ed. Robert C. Allen. London: Routledge.

Macdonald, Patrick T. (1983). The "dope" on soaps. *Journal of Drug Education* 13(4): 359–69.

Mannes, Marya. (1958). *More in anger.* Philadelphia: J.B. Lippincott.

Miller, Daniel. (1995). The consumption of soap opera: *The Young and the Restless* and mass consumption in Jamaica. In *To be continued...* Ed. Robert C. Allen. London: Routledge.

_____. (Ed.). (1995b). *Worlds apart: Modernity through the prism of the local.* London: Routledge.

Miller, Jean Baker. (1986). *Toward a new psychology of women.* 2nd ed. Boston: Beacon Press.

Miller, Jeffrey. (1986). *Street talk: The language of Coronation Street.* Toronto: CBC Enterprises.

Modleski, Tania. (1982). *Loving with a vengeance: Mass produced fantasies for women.* Hamden, CT: Archon.

Nariman, Heidi N. (1993). *Soap operas for social change: Toward a methodology for entertainment-education television.* Media & Society Series. Westport, CT: Praeger.

Nelson, Scott R. (1992). Pine Valley prostitute: The representation of *All My Children's* Donna Tyler. In *Staying tuned...* Ed. Suzanne Frentz. Bowling Green, OH: Bowling Green State University Popular Press.

Neumann, Deborah. (1983). Setting the mood: soap opera settings and fashions. In *Life on Daytime Television.* Ed. Mary Cassata and Thomas Skill. Norwood NJ: Ablex.

Newcomb, Horace. (1974). *Television: The most popular art.* Garden City, NY: Anchor.

Nochimson, Martha. (1992). *No end to her: Soap opera and the female subject.* Berkeley: University of California Press.

Nown, Graham. (1985). *Coronation Street 1960-1985: Twenty-five Years.* Toronto: CBC Enterprises.

Paterson, Richard. (1981). The production context of *Coronation Street.* In *Coronation Street.* Ed. Richard Dyer et al. London: British Film Institute.

Porter, Dennis. (1977). Soap time: Thoughts on a commodity art form. *College English* 38(8): 782–88.

Powdermaker, Hortense. (1950). *Hollywood, The dream factory: An anthropologist looks at the movie-makers.* 1st ed. Boston: Little, Brown.

Propp, Vladimir. (1968). *Morphology of the folktale.* 2nd. rev.ed. Ed. Louis A. Wagner. Austin, TX: University of Texas Press.

Raddatz, Leslie. (1977). October 15. "Soap opera used to be fun." In *TV Guide.* October 15.

Rofel, Lisa. (1995). The melodrama of national identity in post-Tiananmen China. In *To be continued...* Ed. Robert C. Allen. London: Routledge.

Rowbotham, Sheila. (1979). The trouble with patriarchy. *New Statesman.* December 21-28.

Shapiro, Laura. (1995). Do women like to cook? *Granta* 52 (Winter): 153–62.

Silverman, Deborah L., Mary Cassata, and Thomas Skill. (1983). Setting the mood: An analysis of the music of *General Hospital* and *As the World Turns.* In *Life on daytime television.* Ed. Mary Cassata and Thomas Skill. Norwood, NJ: Ablex.

Spence, Louise. (1995). "They killed off Marlena, but she's on another show now": Fantasy, reality, and pleasure in watching daytime soap operas. In *To be continued...* Ed. Robert C. Allen. London: Routledge.

Stedman, Raymond W. (1977). *The serials: Suspense and drama by installment.* 2nd ed. Norman, OK: University of Oklahoma Press.

Sutherland, John C., and Shelley J. Siniawsky (1982). The treatment and resolution of moral violations on soap operas. *Journal of Communications* 32(2): 67–74.

Thurber, James. (1948). "Soapland." In *The beast in me and other animals.* New York: Harcourt, Brace.

Wallack, Lawrence, Warren Breed, and James R. De Foe. (1985). Alcohol and soap operas: Drinking in the light of day. *Journal of Drug Education* 15(4): 365–79.

Warren, Tony. (1969). *I was Ena Sharples' father.* London: Duckworth.

Williams, Carol T. (1992). *"It's time for my story": Soap opera sources, structure, and response.* Media & Society Series. Westport, CT: Praeger.

Magazines

Daytime TV. Sterling's Magazines, New York City, NY.

New York Special Edition. *1996 Soap Opera Almanac* 26(6), 1996

Soap Opera Digest. K-Ill Magazines, New York City, NY

Soap Opera Magazine. SOM Publishing, Lantana, FL

Soap Opera Stars. Sterling's Magazines, New York City, NY

Soap Opera Update. Bauer Magazine L.P., Englewood Cliffs, NJ

Soap Opera Weekly. K-Ill Magazines, New York City, NY

The Street Newsletter. Box 108, Toronto, ON M4E 1H2

Yes! (Coronation Street Special Souvenir Edition). London, 1995

Personal Interviews

CANADA AUGUST 1991

Elton, Harry. First executive producer of *Coronation Street*. Ottawa. (By telephone from St. John's).
Eplin, Tom. Actor (Jake MacKinnon, *AW*). Toronto.
Farrell, Sharon. Actor (Flo Webster, *Y&R*). Toronto.
Filewod, Alan. Professor of drama, University of Guelph. St. John's.
Kazer, Beau. Actor (Brock Reynolds, *Y&R*). Toronto.
Novakovitch, Lilana. Canadian agent. Toronto.
Williams, Tonya Lee. Actor (Olivia Hastings, *Y&R*). Toronto.

NEW YORK CITY, SEPTEMBER 1991

Berlin, Meredith. Editor-at-large. *Soap Opera Digest*.
Brookes, Jacqueline. Actress and acting teacher.
Brown, Kale. Actor (Michael Hudson, *AW*).
Burke, Bobby. Set designer, *AW.*
Dano, Linda. Actor (Felicia Gallant, *AW*).
Delgado, Maggie. Costume director, *AW.*
Hammer, Jay. Actor (Fletcher Reade, *GL*).
Rosenberg, Al. Vice-president and editorial director, Sterling's Magazines (publisher of *Soap Opera Stars* and *Daytime TV*).
Stuart, Anna. Actor (Donna Love, *AW*).
Swajesky, Donna. Head writer, *AW.*

ENGLAND, MARCH 1992

Ayres, Allan. BBC Television Press Office (interviewed regarding *El Dorado*). London.
Bain, Morag. Producer, *Emmerdale*. Leeds.
Bowler, Norman. Actor (Frank Tate, *Emmerdale*). Leeds.
Brooke, Judy. Actor (formerly Paula Maxwell, *CS*). Salford.
Cochrane, Nicholas. Actor (Andy MacDonald, *CS*). Salford.
Crookes, Philip. Professor of political science and deputy director-general, European Institute for the Media, University of Manchester. Manchester.
Dawn, Elizabeth. Actor (Vera Duckworth, *CS*). Salford.
Elliot, Tom. Scriptwriter, *CS*. Salford.
Hynes, Fraser. Actor (Joe Sugden, *Emmerdale*). Leeds.
Little, Daran. Archivist, *CS*. Salford.

O'Rourke, Pat. Pub owner, casting agent, and creator of *Lifeboys*. Shipperies Pub, Liverpool. O'Rourke family and *Lifeboys* actors. Shipperies Pub, Liverpool.

Reynolds, Carolyn. Executive producer, *CS*. Salford.

Ross, Jeff. Photographer, Picture Agency. Leeds.

Spence, Phil. Photographer, *The Daily Mirror*. Leeds.

Tarmey, Bill. Actor (Jack Duckworth, *CS*) Salford.

Tattersall, Mark. Photographer, *The Sun*. Leeds.

Turner, Katy. Press officer, Yorkshire Television. Leeds.

Warren, Tony. Novelist and original writer of *CS*. Salford/Manchester.

Young, Mal. Producer, *Brookside*. Liverpool.